SIRKKA-LIISA KONTTINEN

The Tate Photography Series is a celebration of international and British photography in the Tate collection and an introduction to some of the most significant photographers at work today.

Each book focuses on an individual photographer and features a specially selected sequence of photographs, an introduction by a Tate curator, and a conversation with the photographer. These collaborations between living artists and experts enrich our understanding of photography and its connection to everyday life, and move from city streets to seashores, across landscapes and subcultures, through identities and interiors, in a visual travelogue of our world today.

Set against the various social, political and cultural issues of our time, the theme for Series One is Community and Solidarity, which brings together four photographers, unrelated as individual artists yet unified here by their work. A Ghanaian-Russian photographer joins Black Lives Matter street protests in London, an artist-activist in New Delhi chronicles women's emancipatory struggles, a South-African's camera locates queer lives in rural townships, while a Finnish-British photographer captures the community spirit in the North-East of England as perhaps only an émigré can.

Work from several continents is brought together, connected by shared practice. In all of these locations and environments, each imbued with unique struggles and dangers, a commonality of human character and strength inspired by community and solidarity is portrayed, permitting glimpses of joy and hope.

Series One

1:1   **LIZ JOHNSON ARTUR**
1:2   **SIRKKA-LIISA KONTTINEN**
1:3   **SABELO MLANGENI**
1:4   **SHEBA CHHACHHI**

SIRKKA-LIISA KONTTINEN

Edited by
Thomas Kennedy

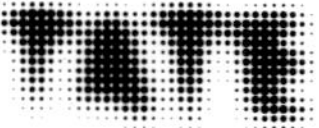

First published 2022 by order of the Tate Trustees
by Tate Publishing, a division of Tate Enterprises Ltd,
Millbank, London SW1P 4RG
www.tate.org.uk/publishing

A catalogue record for this book is available from
the British Library

ISBN 978 1 84976 800 9

Distributed in the United States and Canada
by ABRAMS, New York

Library of Congress Control Number applied for

Series Editors: Simon Armstrong and Yasufumi
Nakamori
Senior Editor: Nicola Bion
Production: Bill Jones
Picture Research: Emma O'Neill
Designed by Sarah Boris
Colour reproduction by Westerham Press, London
Printed and bound in the UK by Westerham Press,
London

Front cover: *Girl on a Spacehopper (Byker)* 1971
(see p.21)
Back cover top: *Jimmy Dodds, Albion Row Allotments
(Byker)* 1980 (see p.29)
Back cover bottom: *Whitley Bay, June* 1989 (see p.55)

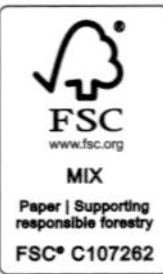

CONTENTS

INTRODUCTION

This publication explores themes of community through the photographic practice of Sirkka-Liisa Konttinen by comparing two series, *Byker* (1969–83) and *Writing in the Sand* (1978–98). Her series *Byker* captures a working-class neighbourhood and reveals the devastating impact that the redevelopment of Newcastle's East End had on the local community. In *Writing in the Sand*, Konttinen turns her attention to the local coast as a place for freedom and leisure. The series is a celebration of spontaneous games, leisurely strolls and jubilant group outings encountered on the beaches of North East England. By comparing the two series, the publication conveys a broad and multifaceted narrative of life in northern England.

Sirkka-Liisa Konttinen was born in Myllykoski, municipality of Sippola, Finland, in 1948. She studied filmmaking at the Regent Street Polytechnic in London in 1960s before founding the Amber Film & Photography Collective with her fellow students and moving to the North of England. Based in Newcastle, she has created several photographic series including *Byker* (1983), *The Hoppings* (1971), *Interiors* (1981), *Step by Step* (1987), *Writing in the Sand* (2000), *The Coal Coast* (2003) and *Byker Revisited* (2009). Together with her partner Peter Roberts at the Amber collective she made several award-winning photo films, the first of which was *Byker*. Her photographs and Amber's films were inscribed in the British section of the UNESCO Memory of the World Register in 2011.

Her work has been included in several displays and exhibitions including the *After Industry: Communities in Northern England 1960s–1980s* collection display at Tate Britain (2021–2); *Facing Britain,*

Kunsthalle Darmstadt, Germany (2021); *Women Photographers from The AmberSide Collection*, Stills, Edinburgh (2019–20); *Home Sweet Home 1970-2018: The British Home, A Political History*, Les Rencontres de la Photographie, Arles, France (2019); *About the North: Imagined Dialogues*, Side Gallery, Newcastle upon Tyne (2018); *Byker / Living Cities*, Tate Modern, London (2016); *The Hoppings & Byker Revisited*, L. Parker Stephenson Photographs, New York (2015); *Work Rest and Play, Half a Century of British Photography*, Misheng Art Museum, Shanghai, and touring (2015); and *For Ever Amber*, Laing Art Gallery, Newcastle upon Tyne (2015).

Thomas Kennedy
Assistant Curator, Modern British Art, Tate

SIRKKA-LIISA KONTTINEN AND THOMAS KENNEDY IN CONVERSATION

TK Taking your career back to the beginning, can you talk about your early life?

SLK I was born and grew up in Finland, in a place called Myllykoski, a small papermill town. My passion for photography was kindled when I was twelve years old and I borrowed a camera from my Aunt Oili, who had an eye for spontaneous moments in my family's life. I wanted to test if the camera could capture the sparkles in the snow. A year later, I won a drawing competition in a children's magazine, with a prize of 365 chocolate bars, one for each day of the year. I carried the boxes to my local shop and persuaded the shopkeeper to buy them from me. With that money I bought my first enlarger. I had already saved up for a camera, so I took a train to the nearest town and joined a camera club, where I was taught to process film and to print by the other members, kind middle-aged men.

When my family acquired a television set in the mid-1960s, I saw a programme about the work of six Finnish documentary photographers, all men of course, and I immediately identified myself as belonging among them.

After leaving school I hounded a fashion photographer whose pictures I saw in a women's magazine, urging him to take me on as an apprentice until he eventually relented. Later I interviewed for a training course at the Finnish state television Yleisradio, but I was told, 'You are so young, go out in the world first and then come back.' Wanting to get out into the world anyway, I applied to Helsinki University and – after first passing the obligatory Latin exam – I began my courses in English Language and Theory of Music, and I already had my sights on a film school in London.

During a trip to Poland with an aspiring English filmmaker, I'd had a guided tour around the film and TV studios in Warsaw, where the only woman in the industry that I could see was a film editor, so I decided 'that'll be me, then.' I'd been struck by Andrzej Wajda's film *Ashes and*

Diamonds (1958), and I was set on the path that I thought would deliver both a living and the freedom to continue my passion for photography.

TK	But you were also interested in living in the UK?

SLK	I had worked as a chambermaid at Butlins Holiday Camp hotel in Margate and as an au pair in London during my three-month high school summer break. London was where it was at. And I'd fallen in love with the Beatles.

TK	That's fascinating, and all those factors led you to begin studying filmmaking at London's Regent Street Polytechnic. Tell me about that.

SLK	During my first year at film school I was invited to take part in projects by a group of final-year students who were planning to continue working collectively after graduation. Encouraged by Murray Martin, the founder and visionary of the group, I decided to throw in my lot with them. So, I left the film school at the end of my first year there.

TK	But you knew you had to go!

SLK	I had to go! I was totally drawn to the egalitarian philosophy that became the foundation of Amber, to work independently outside the hierarchies of the film industry. We had already made the decision to leave London and planned to look at industrial cities in the North. And we stopped at the first, Newcastle upon Tyne.

TK	What were your first impressions when you moved north?

SLK	The architecture was awe-inspiring, at times almost surreal. On Newcastle Quayside, where the Amber Collective still has its base, every Victorian sandstone building and all the bridges were black with soot from coal fires, and the River Tyne stank with sewage. Further down the river, the biggest supertankers in the world were being built at the end of a residential street in Wallsend, looming high above the houses, and the giant cranes moved alongside the river like dinosaurs. All this stirred me deeply. Murray used to say that there was nothing in art that came even close to this, the scale and the visual power of it.

TK	And what were the early aims of Amber when it was formed in 1968? Did you set out to document life in Newcastle and engage with the community?

SLK   We didn't consider ourselves to be historians or recorders of social
        change, but of course the early work was very much a celebration
        of the industries that were still present – shipbuilding, mining, heavy
        engineering. Fundamentally, it was an engagement with working-
        class culture and communities through individuals and groups
        we became involved with. The plan was to give voice to those
        communities and to tell their stories, from their perception of
        who they are, applying our skills and artistry.

TK   Who were the other filmmakers and photographers involved in Amber
        at the beginning?

SLK   Murray Martin had grown up in Stoke-on-Trent, in the potteries, and it
        was Murray who had the vision of an artists' collective in dialogue with
        the communities it lives in. Peter Roberts, Graham Smith, Graham
        Denham, Lorna Powell, Pat McCarthy, as well as others who came
        later, were from similar backgrounds. We all felt strongly that working-
        class culture was badly represented by the British media at the time.

TK   A few years after Amber was formed, you also opened Side Gallery
        in Newcastle. How did that come about?

SLK   In the 1960s, documentary photography was not seen as an artform
        in this country and there wasn't a gallery in Newcastle prepared to
        show any photography at all, so for us there was clearly a need to
        put that right. Amber established Side Gallery in 1977 and we still
        run it ourselves. Chris Killip came into it for a while and together
        with Murray brough an international dimension to it. The gallery was
        dedicated to socially engaged documentary photography, and several
        photographers came to be associated with it in various ways through
        Side's commissions and exhibitions. Graham Smith photographed
        extensively in Middlesbrough. Izabela Jedrzejczyk made her *Jungle
        Portraits* in a bar locally known as The Jungle on North Shields
        fish quay. Markéta Luskačová shot on Whitley Bay beach and also
        photographed children's marching kazoo bands known as Juvenile
        Jazzbands, as did Tish Murtha, who continued her dedicated work
        in Elswick, championing her own community there. Chris Killip did
        his work in the region, and bigger group projects engaged more
        photographers. Our ambition at Side was for photographers to be fully
        funded to work on their long-term projects, and the gallery used a
        substantial part of its annual budget towards this aim.

TK   And because of this programme, Side has a very large collection now!

SLK   Yes, thousands of prints and transparencies and a hundred or more
        films. Murray began building the archive from the very first day.
        The agreement with photographers funded by Side was that they
        would leave a set of prints in the archive – not just one or two, but the
        complete story, so the narrative would stay with that work. And it is
        in constant use as a resource and inspiration for new work in schools
        through the Amber Education programmes.

        In 2011 Amber's films and my photographs were inscribed in the
        UNESCO UK Memory of the World Register as 'being of outstanding
        national value and importance to the United Kingdom', and the
        AmberSide Trust, set up in 2015 will continue to secure the Collection
        in its integrity for present and future generations.

TK   Amber is one of the longest lasting film and photography collectives
        in Britain. Working through the deindustrialisation and the
        unemployment at the time it was founded is quite an achievement.
        And it sounds, from the way you talk about it, so organic.

SLK   The egalitarian principles we set up at the beginning certainly lasted
        – for nearly fifty years, in fact. We pooled our individual earnings
        to provide the workshop rent, the equipment, and an equal wage
        for all and I think we survived largely because of that. Initially I did
        some rather odd jobs to contribute to the pool, including a spell at
        waitressing and go-go dancing in a black catsuit at a local night club,
        for £1 a night! Our first living wage at Amber in the early 1970s was £8
        a week. It took me six years to pay off my loans for a year at Helsinki
        University and a year at Regent Street Polytechnic, now the University
        of Westminster in London – mostly with Murray's winnings on horse
        races. Eventually we came to own our own buildings and the shared
        economy certainly enabled me to sustain my photography
        in Byker and for the group to maintain a degree of stability.

        By the 1980s Amber was at the forefront of forging the radical
        Workshop Agreement with the Film and Television Union ACTT and
        the BFI along with other independent film collectives in the UK,
        and as a franchised workshop we were funded by Channel 4 television
        to make our own work, which kept us going for more than a decade.
        This was followed by a number of commissions from the BBC.
        We made documentaries, photo films and dramas, ran Side Gallery
        and Side Cinema, built our own local and international distribution
        networks, and much else besides. At times the collective grew almost
        too big for its own good! We also had trotting horses, a commercial

fishing boat, a pub by a shipyard, an ex-chapel, a café ... part of our projects and as our community bases.

Northern Arts, Newcastle City Council and various foundations have invested in us over the years, resulting in our unparalleled living archive of film and photography. Although Murray Martin died in 2007, and most members from the original group have now retired, AmberSide continues into its second half-century with a younger, committed workforce and a socially engaged vision based on its legacy.

TK   Newcastle itself has been key to both Amber's work and your own. As someone who moved to this country, what was your relationship with local communities when you first arrived in Newcastle?

SLK   The 'Geordie' sociability really struck a chord with me. In Finland, personal space is hugely valued and you try to put a bit of distance between yourself and your neighbour. So, it was quite a surprise when, on my first night out on my own in Byker at the Hare and Hounds pub at the bottom of my street, drinks kept arriving with a welcoming smile and a nod from an assortment of kindly faces around the room. I think I was the only foreigner there at that time and the matronly women in my street took me under their wing, worried that I was too young to be so far away from home. I was totally amazed, people so readily taking me into their community.

TK   And at the time everything was closing – the mines, the shipyards, the heavy industries, all those things that had so struck you when you arrived. And then, due to the urban regeneration schemes by local authorities, your home and the area were getting demolished. What was your experience of that? It must have been just looming on the horizon?

SLK   When we came to Newcastle, each of us needed somewhere to live. I just walked around the area, came across Byker, and that was that – I fell in love with it. I ended up living there for seven years, till my street came down. I wasn't aware of it yet, but even then its total demolition was on the cards – Byker had been scheduled for redevelopment for twenty-five years. A third of it had already been cleared for a motorway, which was never built, and many of the properties had been allowed to run down. Eventually the city settled on Ralph Erskine, a renowned English architect living in Stockholm, who was commissioned to design the new Byker Wall Estate.

TK   Twenty-five years is a long time…

SLK   Those seven years that I lived there, they were really years of loss, you know. People were being moved out and by 1976, when my street came down, all my neighbours had gone. The plans for the Byker Wall Estate looked reasonable enough on paper, with the promise that people would be moved out temporarily while their new homes were being built. You look at the newspapers of that period, and the planners' promise that you could 'move from your old house directly into your new home, next to your old neighbour', was totally implausible but it was a way to win people over. Of course, everyone wanted an indoor toilet and bathroom and central heating, but we could have had all those things if our old homes had just been refurbished. Instead, they pulled the place down and destroyed the community.

TK   Due to the demolition of these housing estates, your home and community, did the feeling of Newcastle change at that time?

SLK   Yes, of course. Architecture has a huge impact. In the grid pattern of the streets in the old Byker and other similar communities with terraced streets, you'd pass your neighbour's door every day and notice if the milk bottle was still on the doorstep after midday, and if it was, you'd knock on the door to check if the old lady inside was okay. There was that sort of knowledge, everybody knowing everybody. 17,000 people were still living in Byker at the start of the redevelopment, and the place had a sense of working networks built over generations. The Byker Wall Estate, with its more idiosyncratic planning with warrens and cul-de-sacs, was offering its residents more privacy but also more potential for isolation.

TK   And because of this seismic change, what does the notion of community mean to you?

SLK   For me, the notion of community in Newcastle is best exemplified by the two Bykers I got to know and became part of. The original Byker community was born around local industries, as generations of families formed strong bonds with their locality and support networks with their neighbours. Twenty-five years later, at the time I re-engaged with Byker, the Byker Wall Estate had become multicultural, almost overnight, when Byker opened a reception centre for refugees and asylum seekers. Today it has an unusually expansive socio-demography for such a small geographic area, with a number of active communities around ethnicity, churches, cultural activities and so on. There is a traditionally strong sense of belonging in people living in the North East and Newcastle, noted for its openness and warmth. As for me, I have lived my entire working life in the Newcastle area and that must speak for itself.

TK   Your photographs from before the demolition do have that sense of a community networking together and of supporting one another. What was it like when you first came to photograph your community and neighbourhood?

SLK   Initially, I think, you would call it street photography. Before I ever thought of a project, I began photographing whatever struck me as beautiful, amazing, worth telling about. After my first couple of years in Newcastle I built a little studio with a darkroom in an abandoned hairdressing salon on the main shopping street in Byker, and mounted my photographs in its window, opposite a busy bus stop. I invited people to sit for a free portrait and to have a chat, and to bring in their own photographs and stories. Willie became one of the regulars, posing with his plastic parrot and a fiddle he couldn't play but loved to be photographed with. A faith healer who 'spoke in tongues' made a daily visit to foretell my troubles and to pray for me. A customer of the long-gone hairdressing salon turned up one day for her portrait with her hair still in a voluminous beehive. Then in 1972 I received the Northern Arts/Northern Gas Board two-year Fellowship in Creative Photography, which was perhaps the biggest photographic award going in the UK at the time. Suddenly I was in the papers and on the telly. That made my project known to everyone in Byker. But then I really felt the need to actually make something of it.

TK   As part of the *Byker* series – shown in the accompanying book and film – you also captured their stories.

SLK   Initially I was just remembering stories and jotting them down as soon as I could. I didn't go around with a tape recorder until much later. Some of the conversations I overheard in shop queues or were given to me as I went around photographing, and of course people eventually invited me into their homes. In all of my work, testimonies have been an important part of the projects. And once all that material was there, turning it into a film was basically arranging the photographs and stories into a narrative, and in the case of the *Byker* film, re-voicing the stories and re-enacting some of the live scenes, because by the time we made the film, Byker had already been pulled down.

TK   Can we talk more about your process of taking photographs – do you feel like you need people's acceptance to take their picture? Has their acceptance resulted in long-term relationships with your subjects?

SLK   Back in the day there was little concern about me walking around in the streets with a camera or being invited into people's homes, or my photographing children. I could not really have posed much of a threat with my camera. In those days there was no social media, so you could not unexpectedly expose someone to the whole world. And if anyone didn't want their picture seen, having spotted the print in my studio window, they would just come to me and say, 'Please take it down.' That only happened once. Mostly people treasured their photographs and thought of me as providing a free service.

As my photography has evolved with every project, working ethically has also evolved alongside, first moving from street photography to negotiated photography and finally to an even more collaborative approach, the one I use in my series *Byker Revisited*.

But looking back to that 'street photography' period, kids out in the streets in Byker were not under an adult eye most of the time and the spreading dereliction gave them a pretty wild adventure playground.

I took a photograph of a girl playing a piano in a house that was virtually left on stilts. There wasn't much there, apart from the staircase to the upstairs flat where she had found a broken piano and began to play it. I was curious about where this sound was coming from and discovered the girl, absorbed in the music she was making. After taking the picture I taught her a little tune and we played it together. I told her, 'If you'd like to, you can pop round sometime and have a play on my piano.' So, she turned up with her little brother a few days later, and she played the tune I had taught her while her little brother went about scanning the flat to see what he could pinch behind my back. I loved these relationships, with all kinds of people in Byker and that was the richness of living and working there.

Long-term relationships – a long-term commitment to the region, and to the particular communities and individuals we have made work with is right at the heart of Amber.

And those relationships begin to have second or third lives by now, you know. People I photographed as children have grown up and are now getting in touch with me to reconnect with their childhoods. And yes, there's a new film, *Still Here*, with some of them looking back at themselves! Amber has always been in Newcastle, so people may have moved away but they know where to find us.

TK Did you ever collaborate with other photographers in Amber? Did you photograph Newcastle or the surrounding area together?

SLK Most of us just did our own thing, but we all felt we were part of something bigger, a kind of collective endeavour. The closest I came to working with another photographer was with London-based Markéta Luskačová. Her partner Chris Killip was working in the region, so Murray suggested that Markéta come up to do a project, and we found her some funding towards her work in Whitley Bay. I had already been photographing the beaches myself intermittently, and for a couple of summers we knocked around together, photographing in our bikinis. She would leave her little boy for a while in the care of any delighted family group, and he was happy while Markéta went about taking her photographs. And then I had a child myself a couple of years later, so we were two young mothers with our babies with us, keeping an eye on each other's while pursuing our projects.

TK Speaking of beaches, I wanted to talk to you about your series *Writing in the Sand*, which grew out of the photographs you'd taken there. The stories of the coast are also so important when looking at communities in the North. In terms of leisure, the sea was a huge part of people's lives.

SLK Absolutely. A lot of people in Byker, including myself, would take the train at weekends to the coast, rain or shine, for a whole day out on the beach. Women organised trips for the children in their streets. Coachloads from inland steel towns and pit villages used to form big circles in corporation deck chairs and tents and then on with rounders and bingo, chasing each other into the sea, burying dad in the sand. Followed by the inevitably sandy sandwiches.

Later, when I lived in Whitley Bay, there was the 'Scottish Fortnight',
an annual workers' holiday from Glasgow and that was big, even
then. Before my time, in the 1950s, till cheap foreign package
holidays began to pull the crowds, three million holidaymakers per
year were visiting Whitley Bay, Cullercoats and Tynemouth, and on
an August Bank Holiday a hundred thousand people would gather
on these beaches.

In my exhibition text for *Writing in the Sand* in 1991 I wrote:
'My daughter, when she was four years old, made an observation:
"It's only half an hour from Newcastle to the beach, but when you're
asleep, it's only half a minute!" In the blink of an eye from the city
to the seaside, and to the freedom that awakens the child in the
toughest of city dwellers.' I think it was on those beautiful sandy
beaches that I really fell in love with the spirit of the people – the
humour, the spontaneous interactions between random parties,
everyone there making the most of their day.

*Based on a conversation between Sirkka-Liisa Konttinen and
Tate Assistant Curator Thomas Kennedy on Friday 16 April 2021
via a video call.*

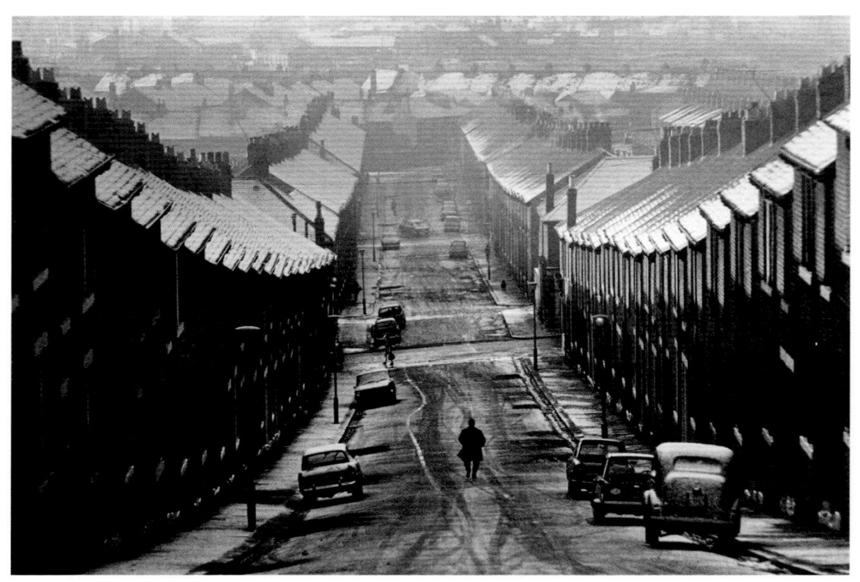

    Kendal Street (Byker) 1969

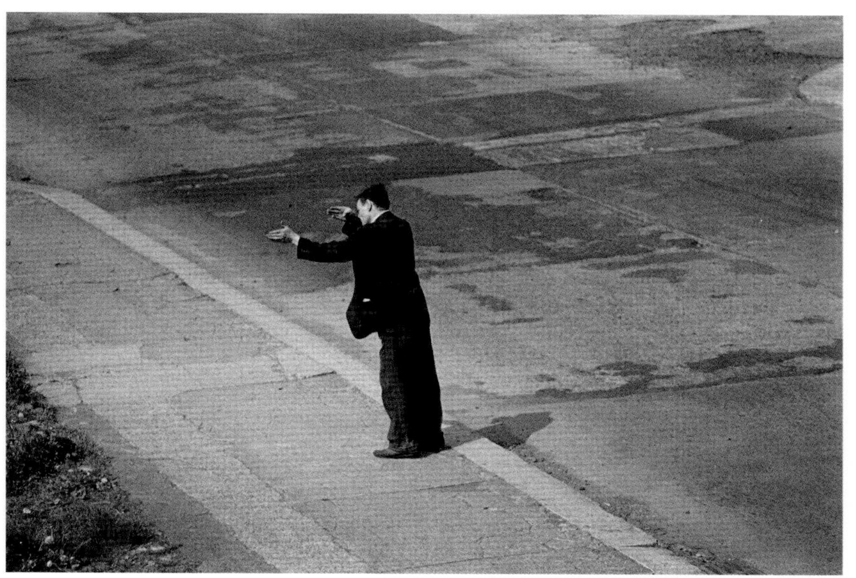

  Man Gesturing in Demolished Street (Byker) 1971

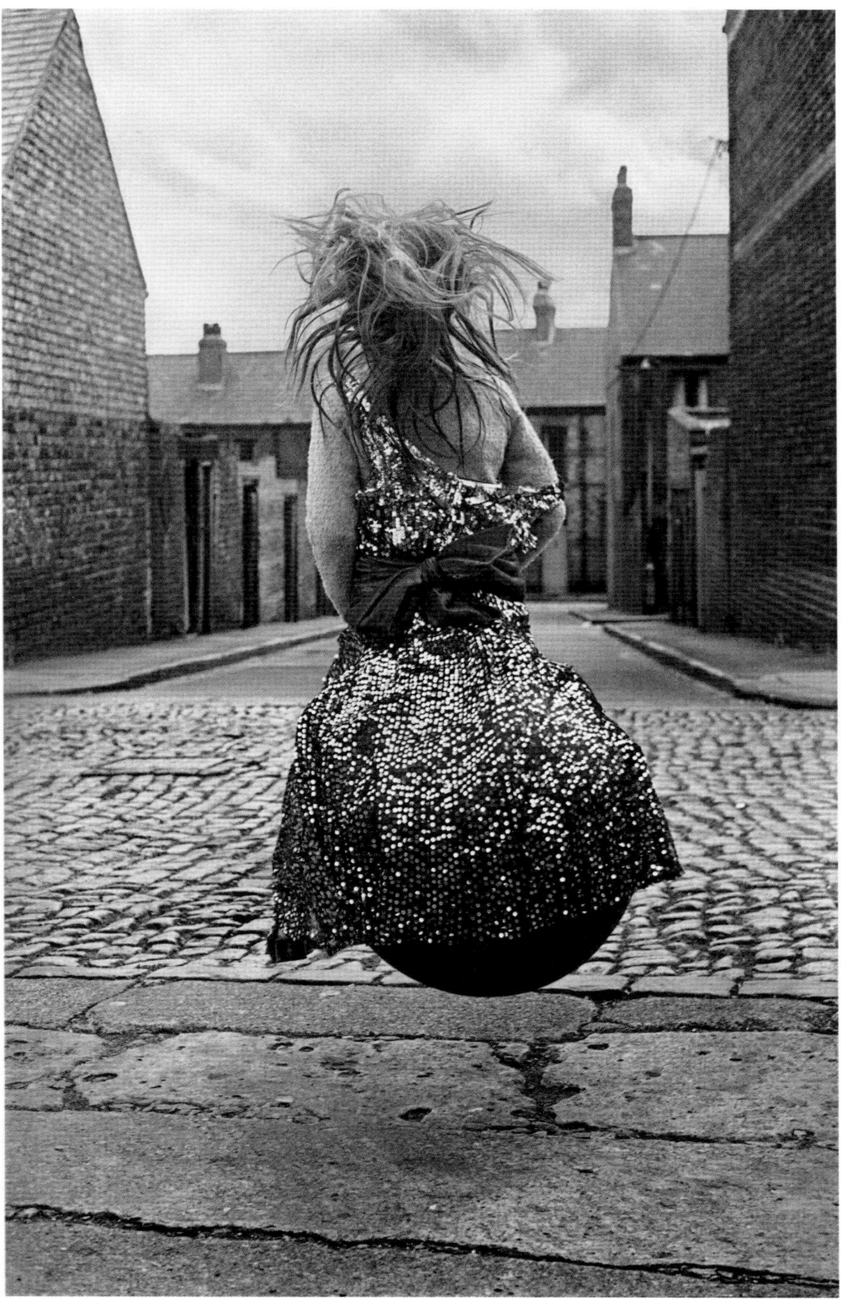

21   *Girl on a Spacehopper (Byker)* 1971

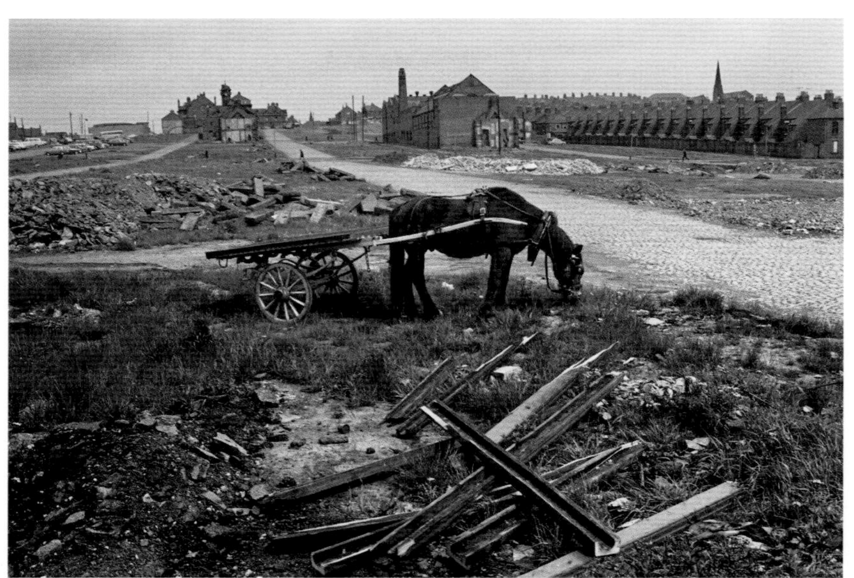

 Ragman's Horse and Cart by Union Road (Byker) 1970

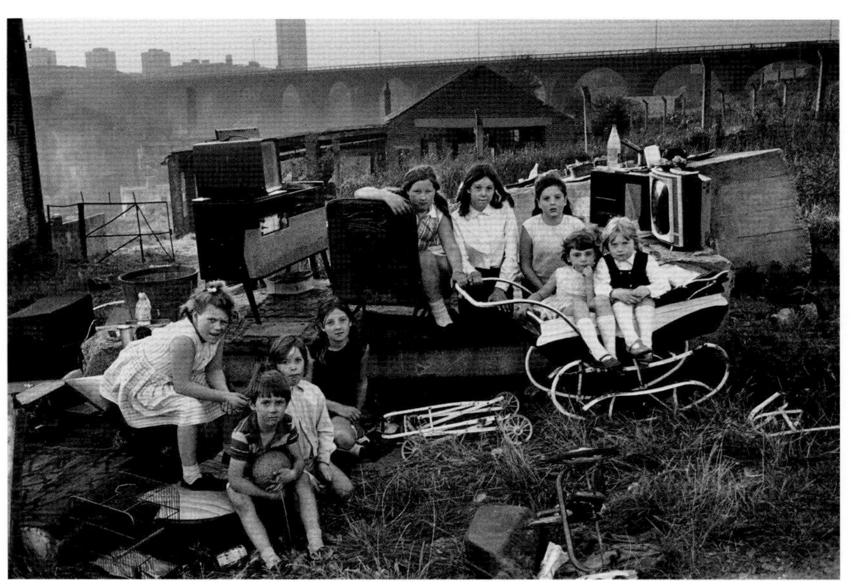

23   *Kids with Collected Junk Near Byker Bridge (Byker)* 1971

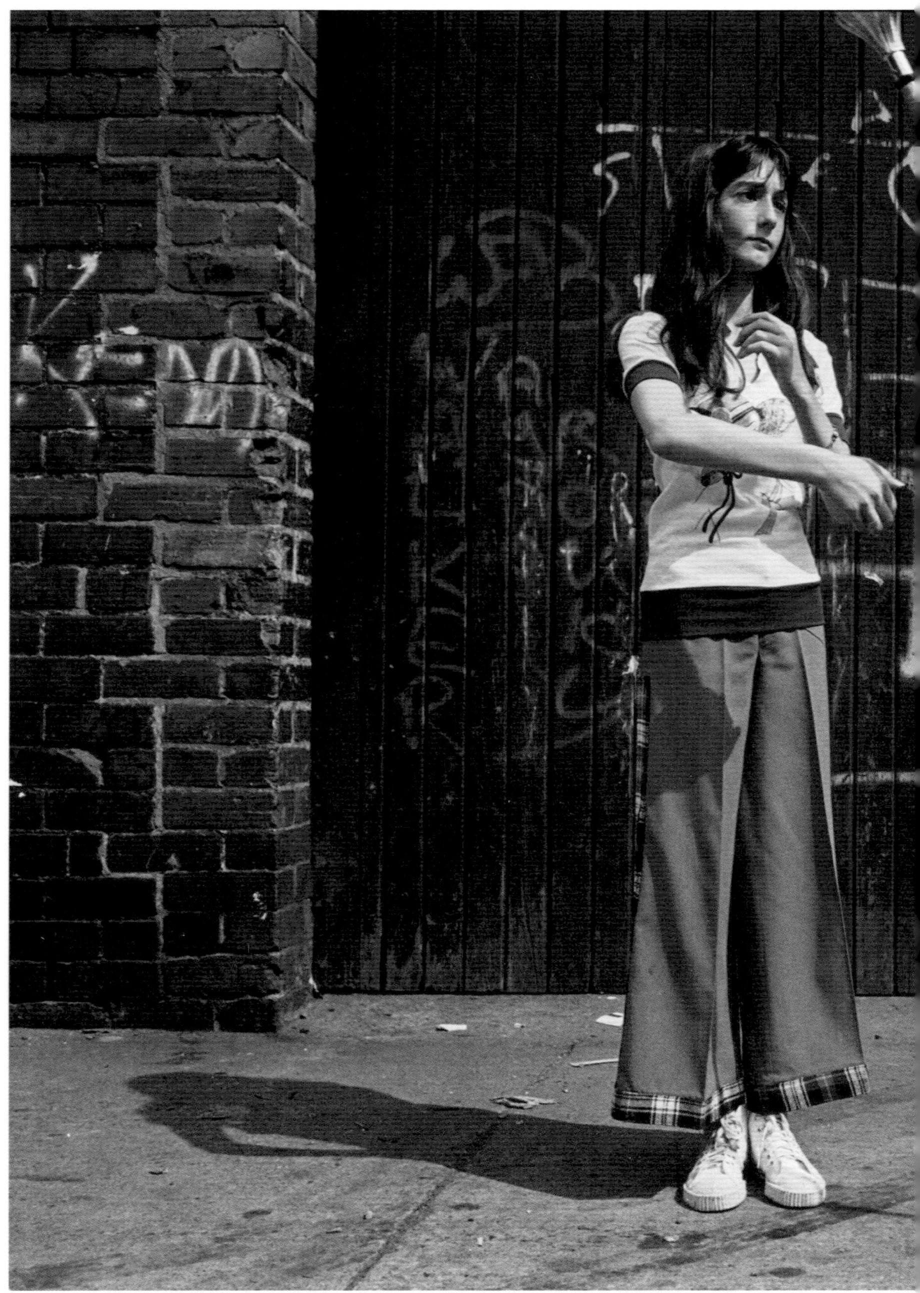

  Girl and toddler practise twirling, Byker 1975

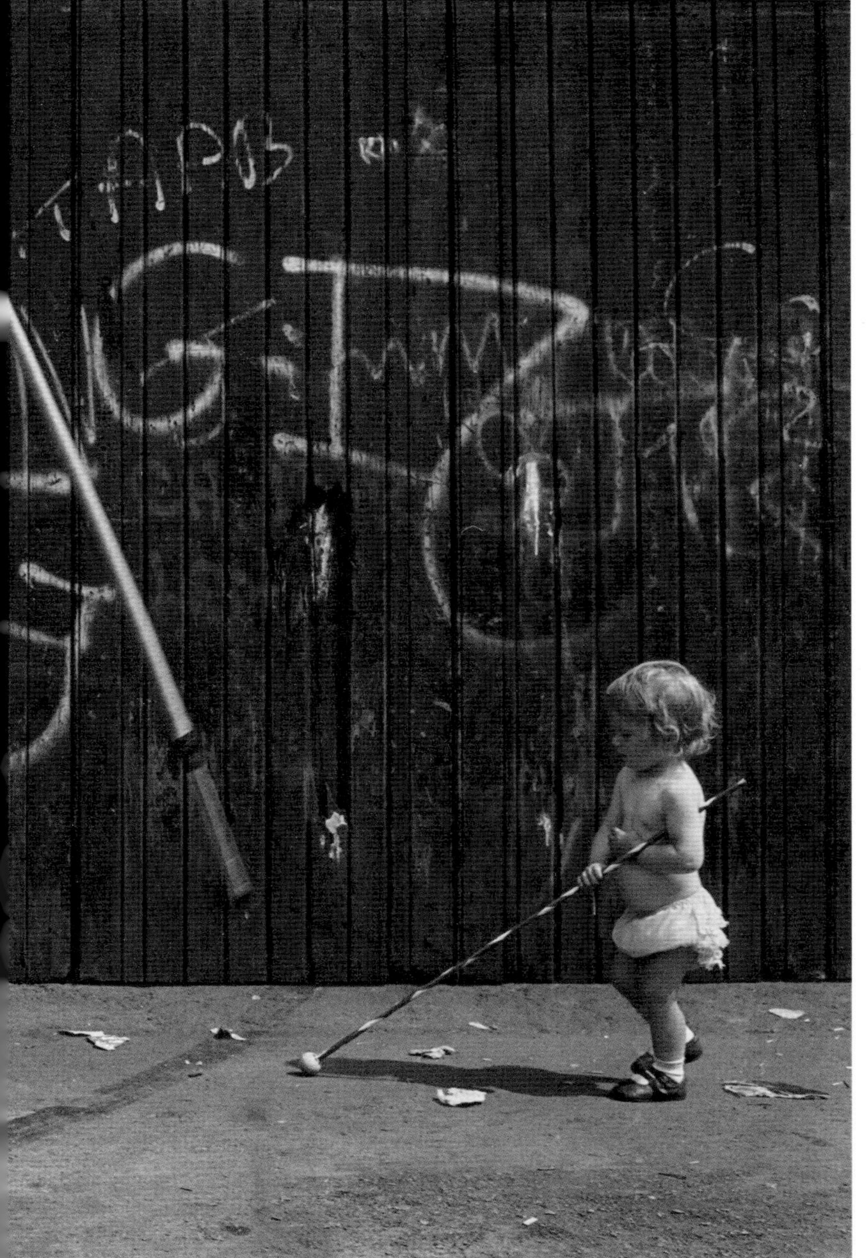

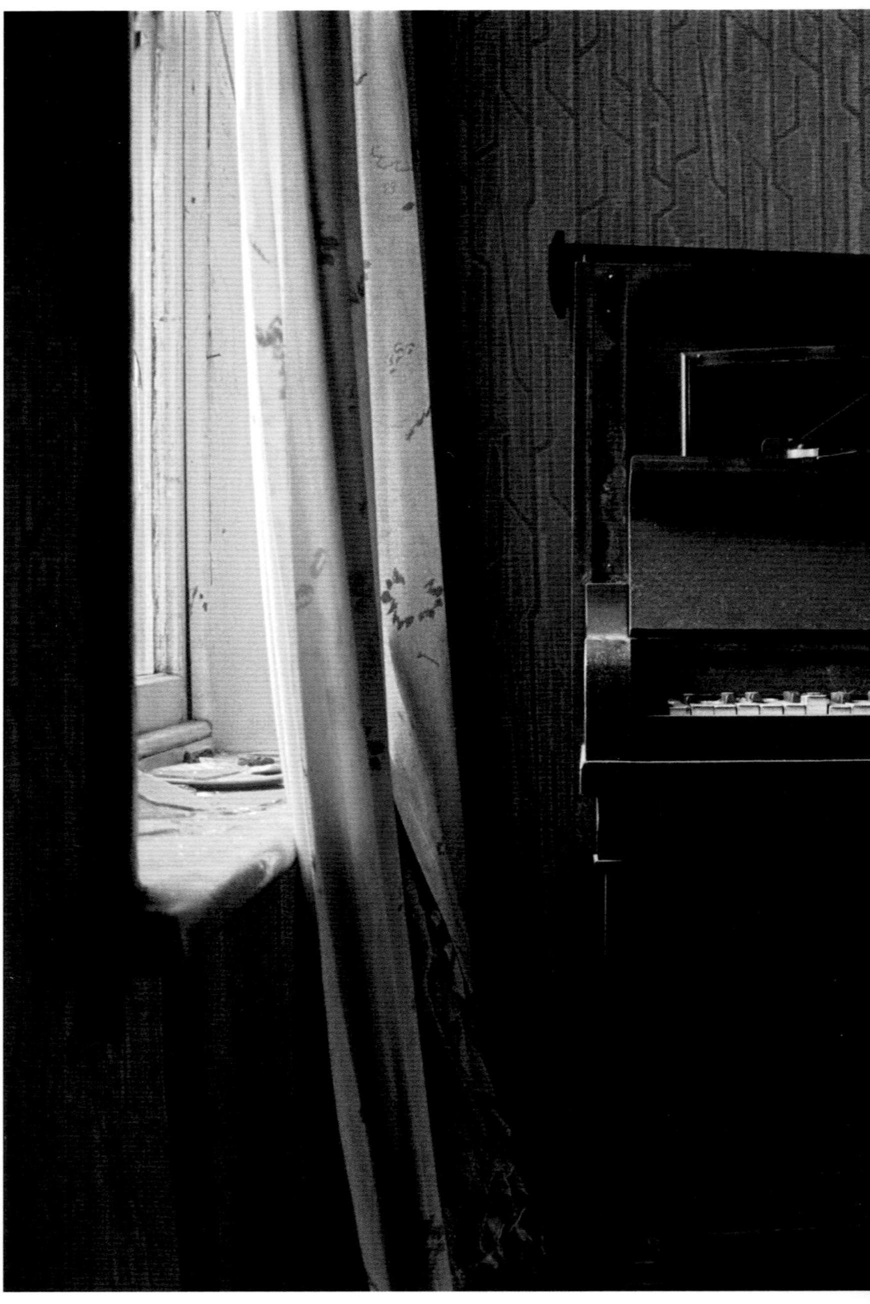

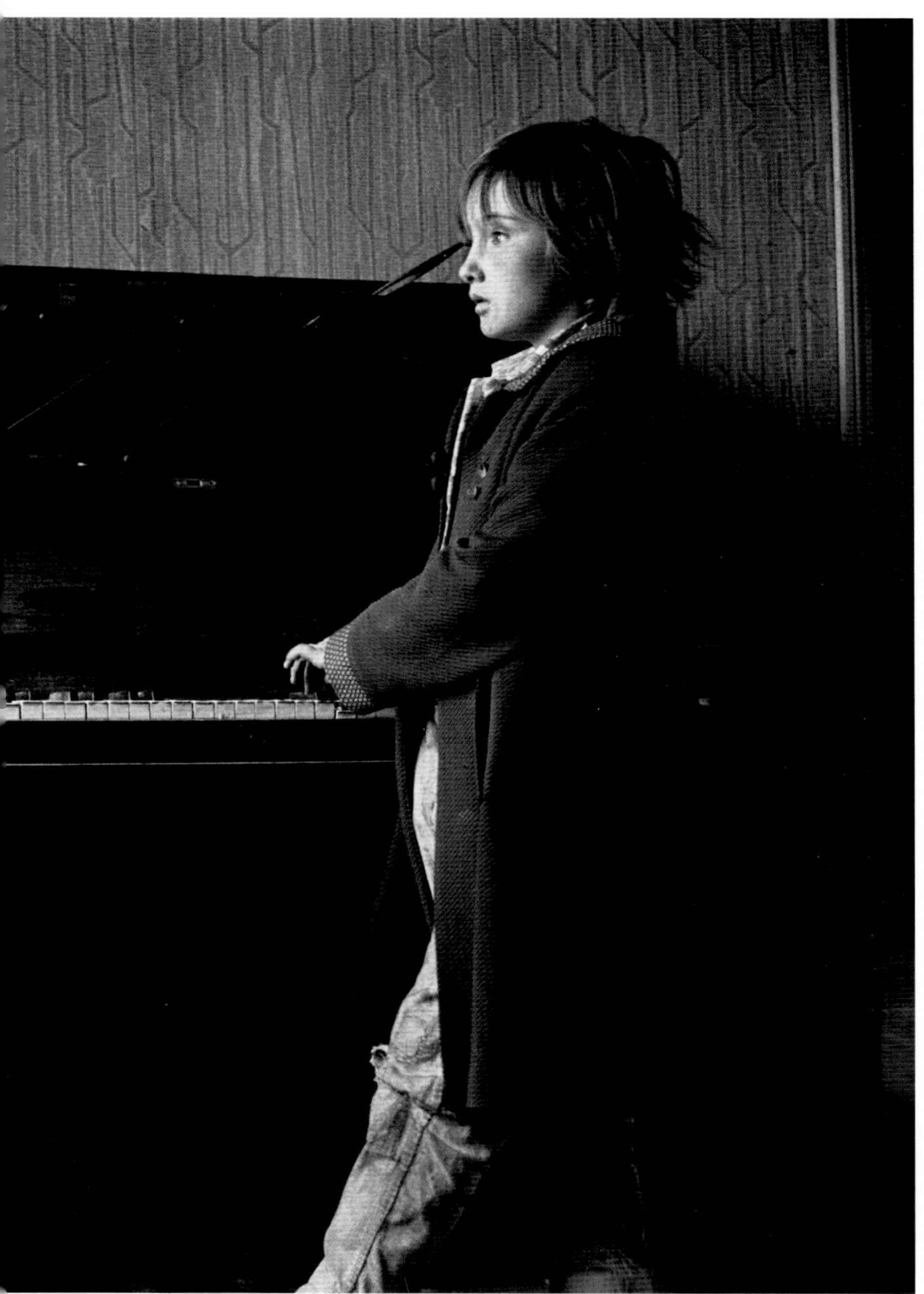

   Heather Playing a Piano in a Derelict House (Byker) 1971

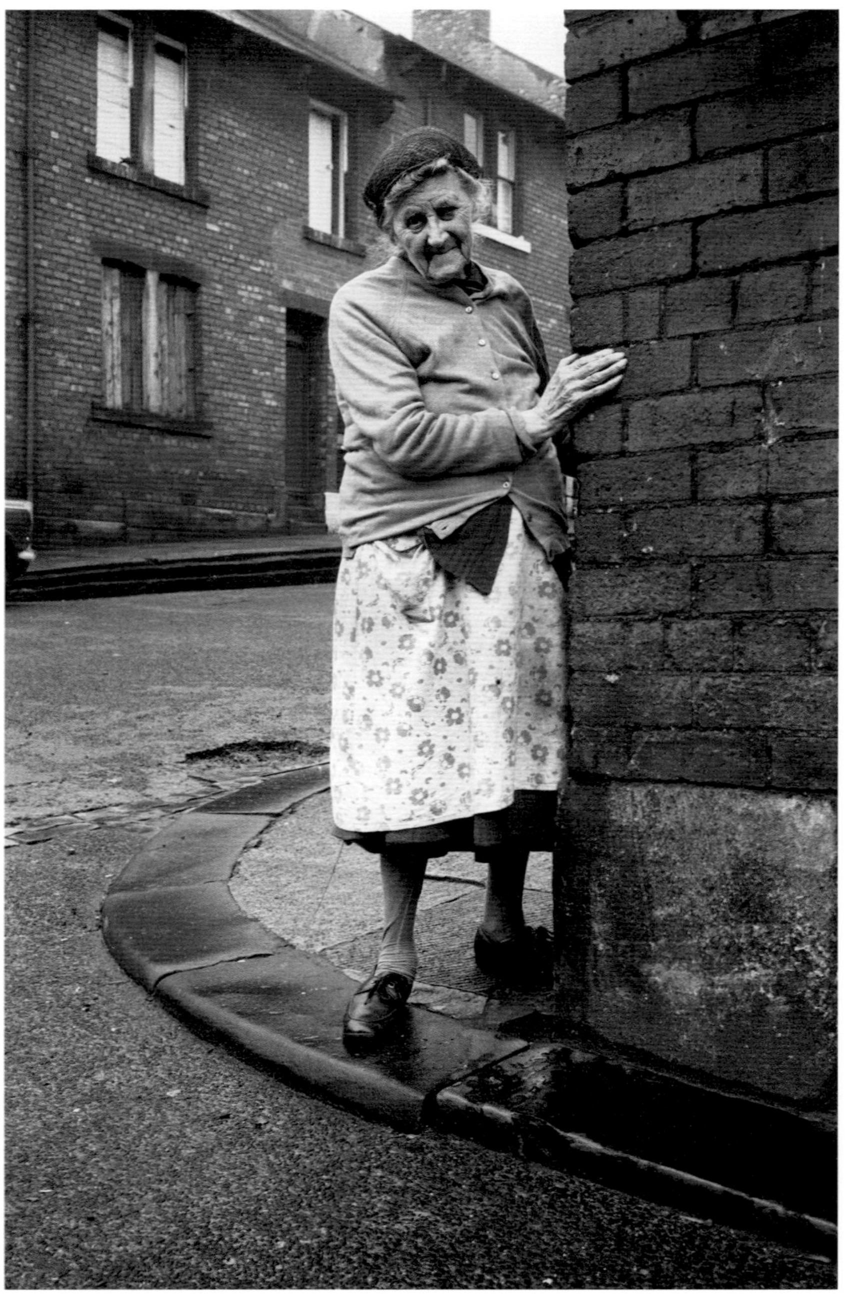

 Mrs Potter in Mason Street (Byker) 1975

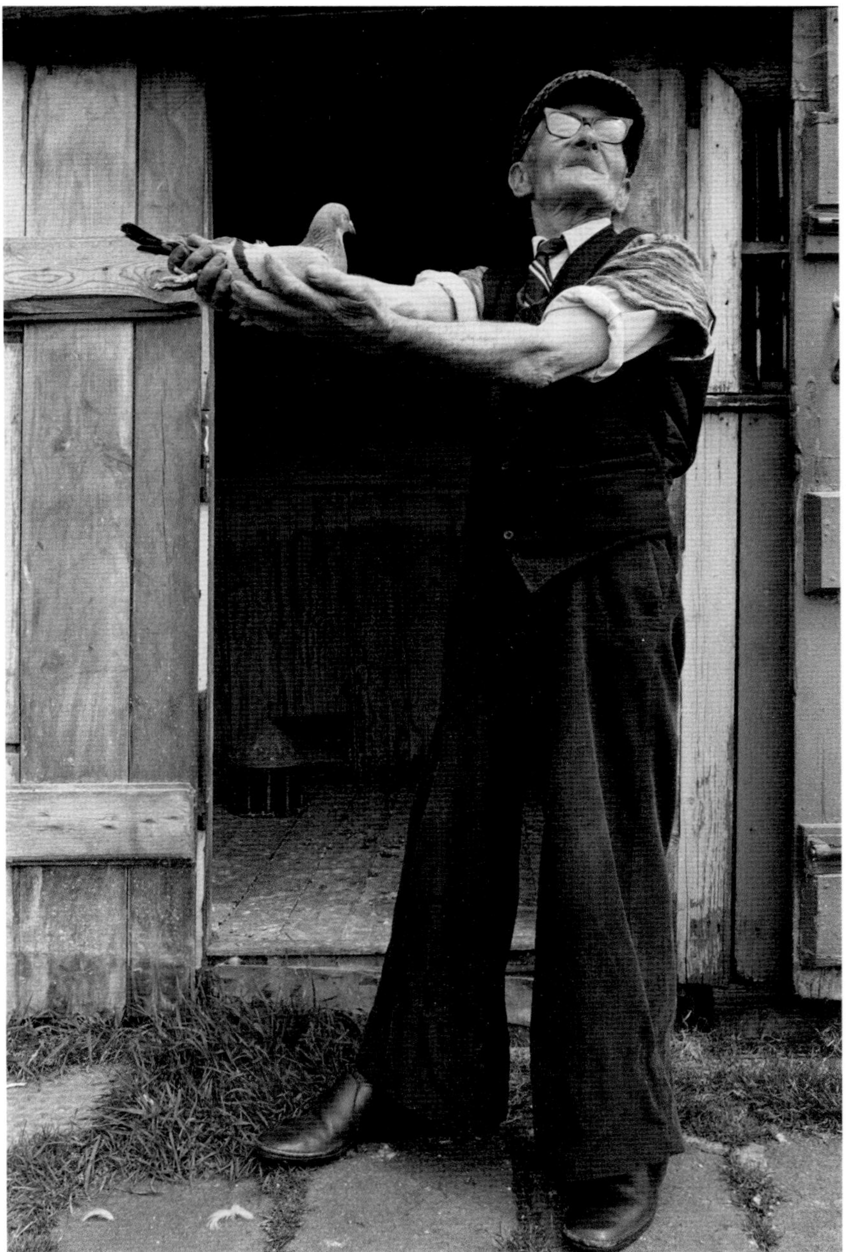

29   *Jimmy Dodds, Albion Row Allotments (Byker)* 1980

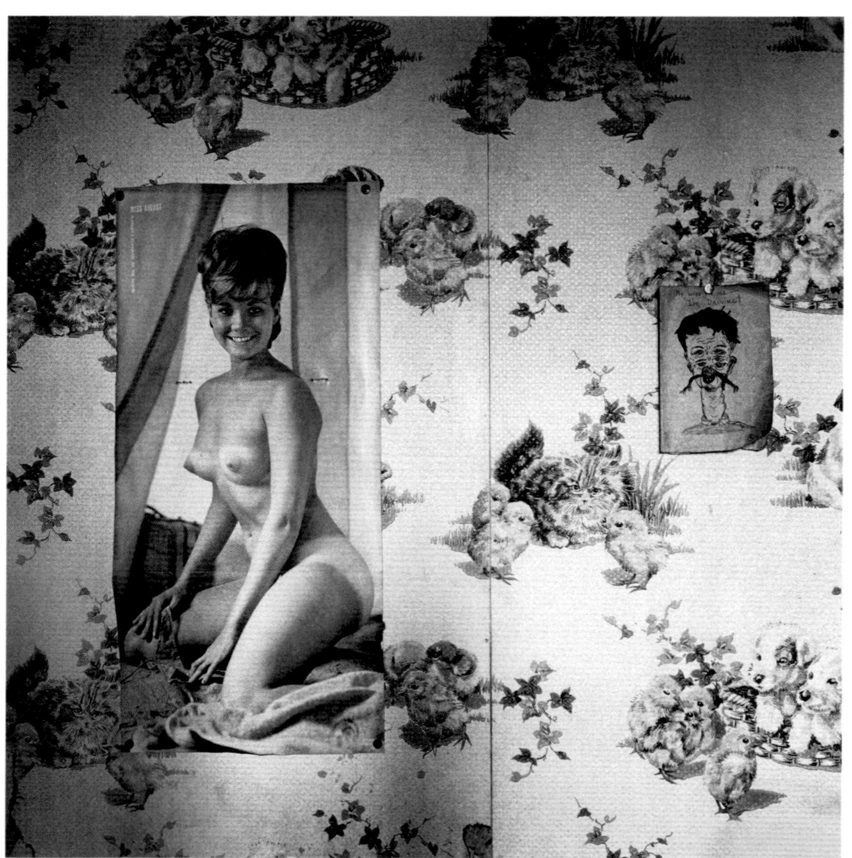

     Living Room Wall of Sidney Aubrey (Byker) 1975

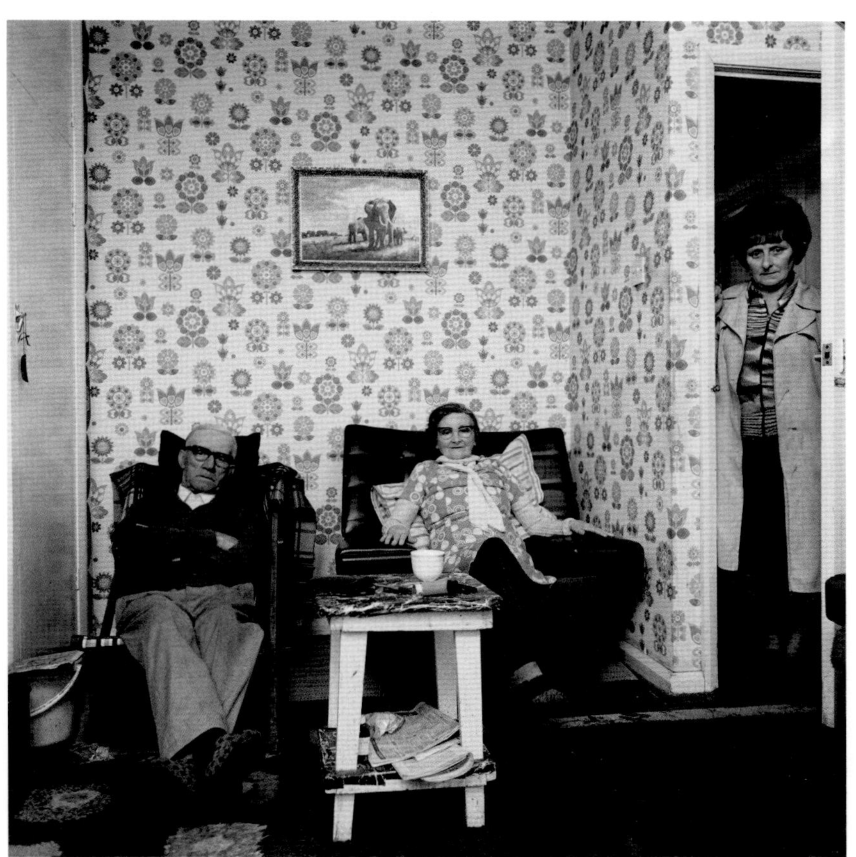

 Jean Barron with Parents (Byker) 1980

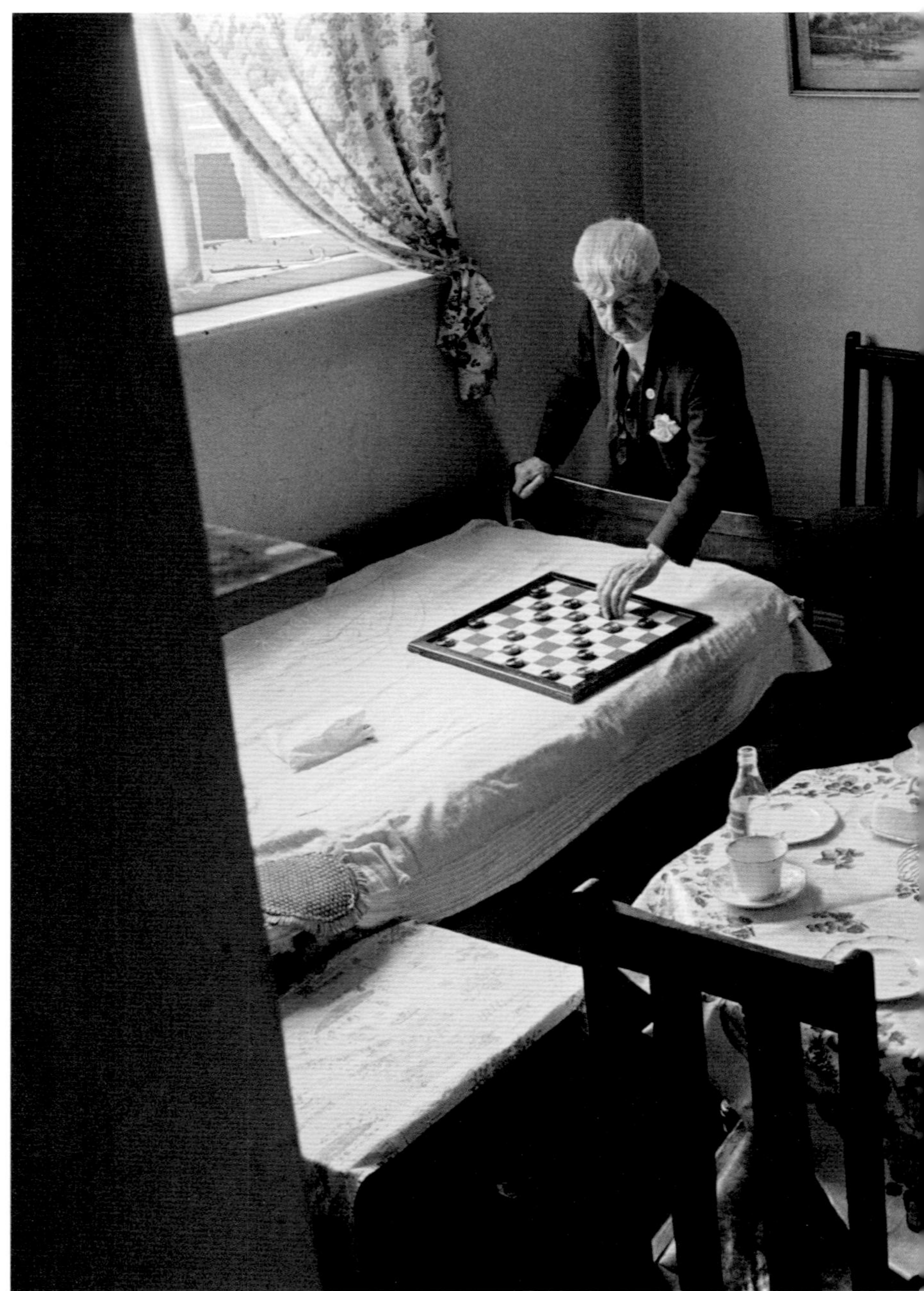

   William Neilson (Byker) 1971

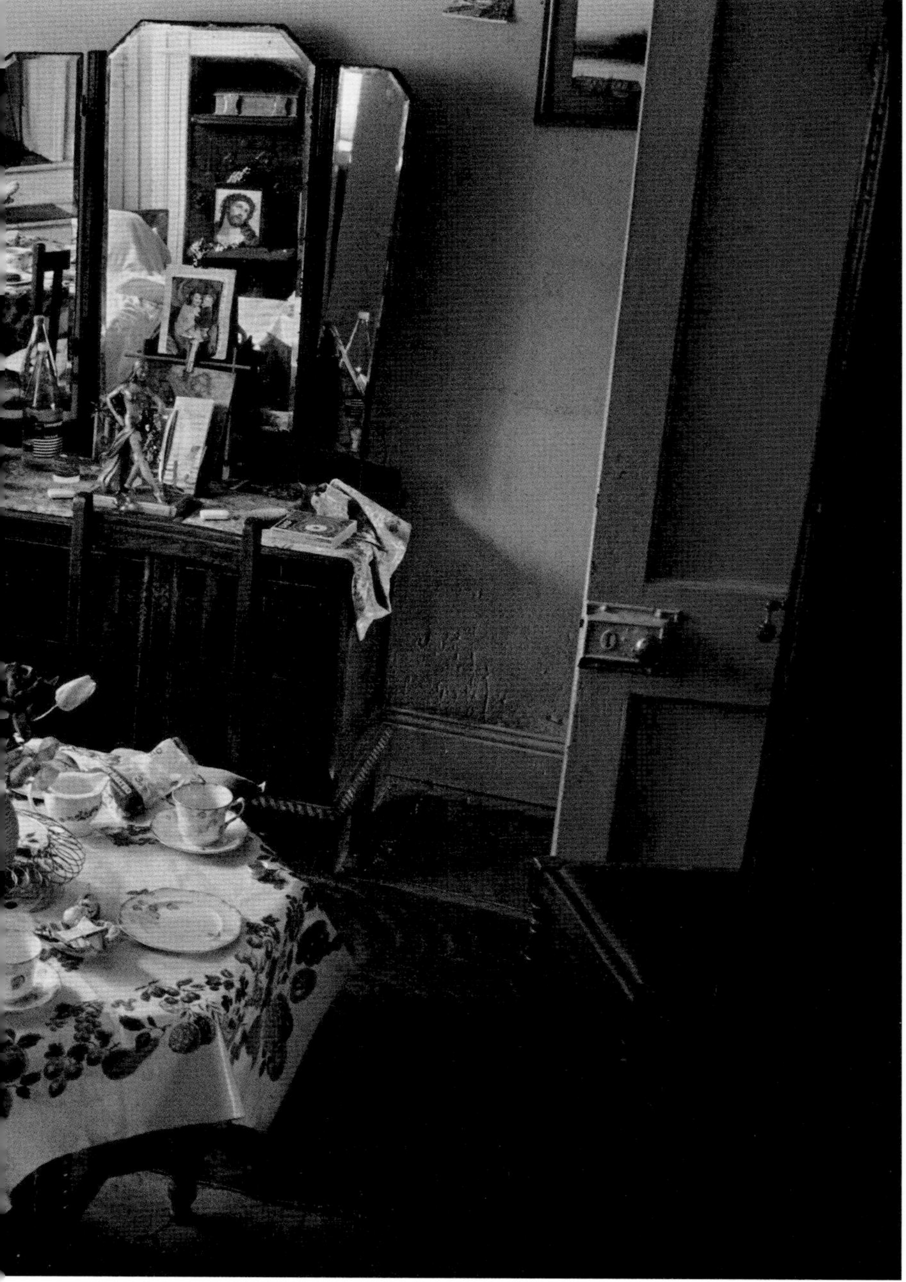

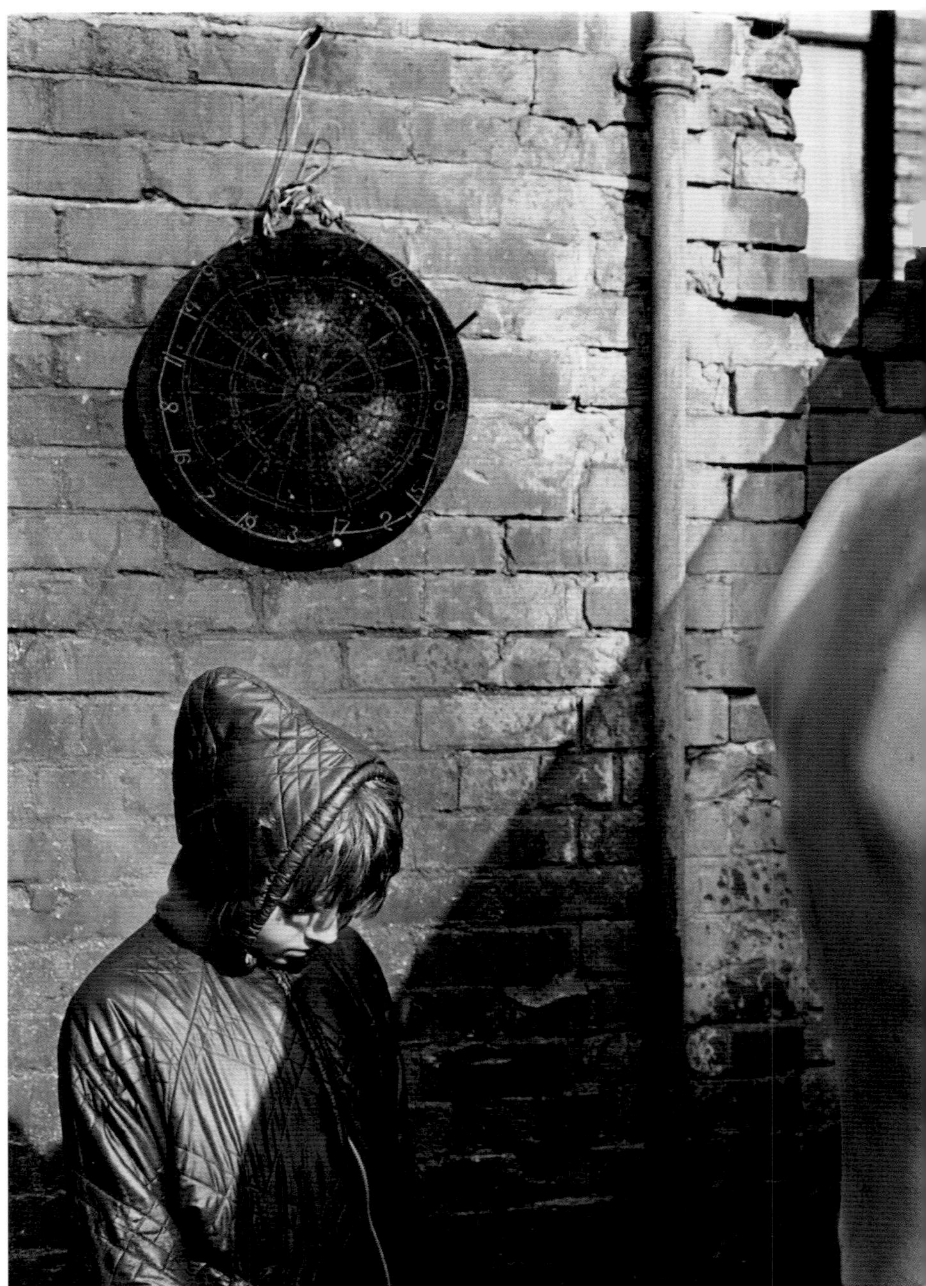

 Young Couple in a Backyard (Byker) 1975

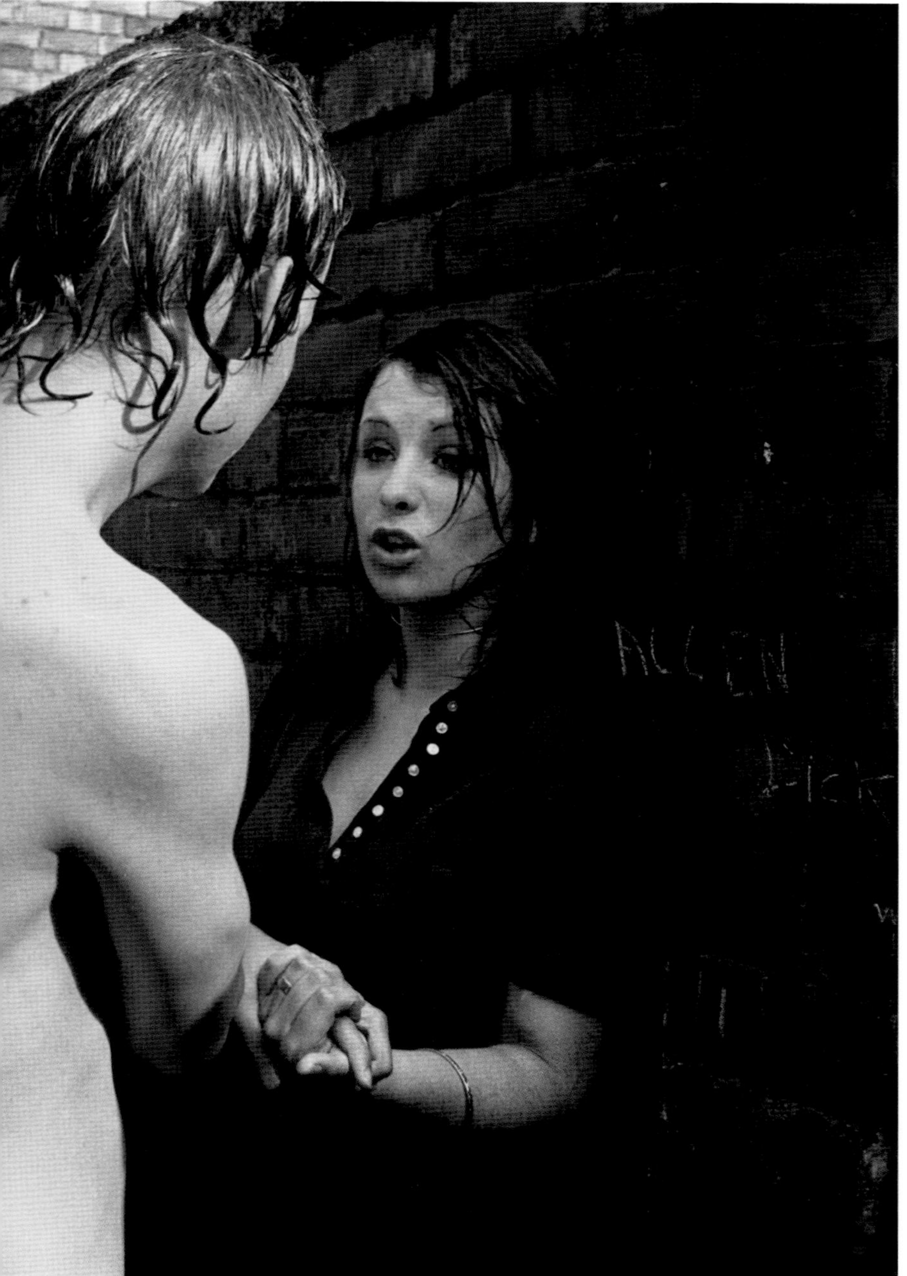

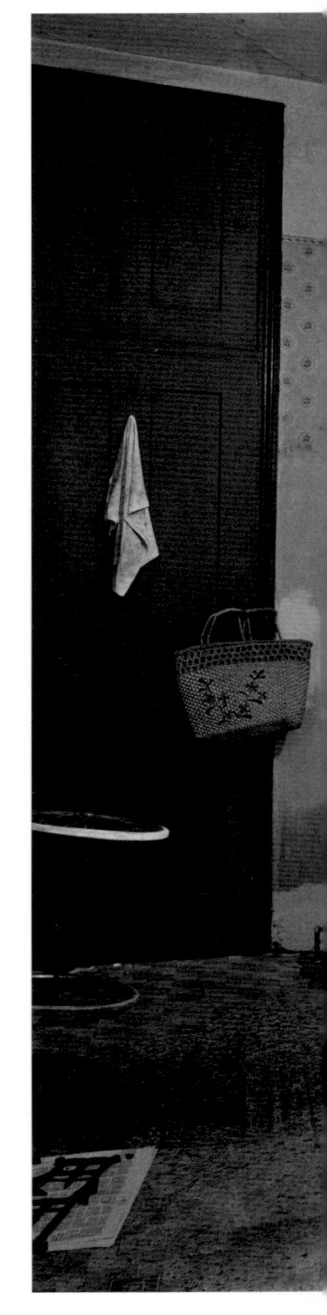

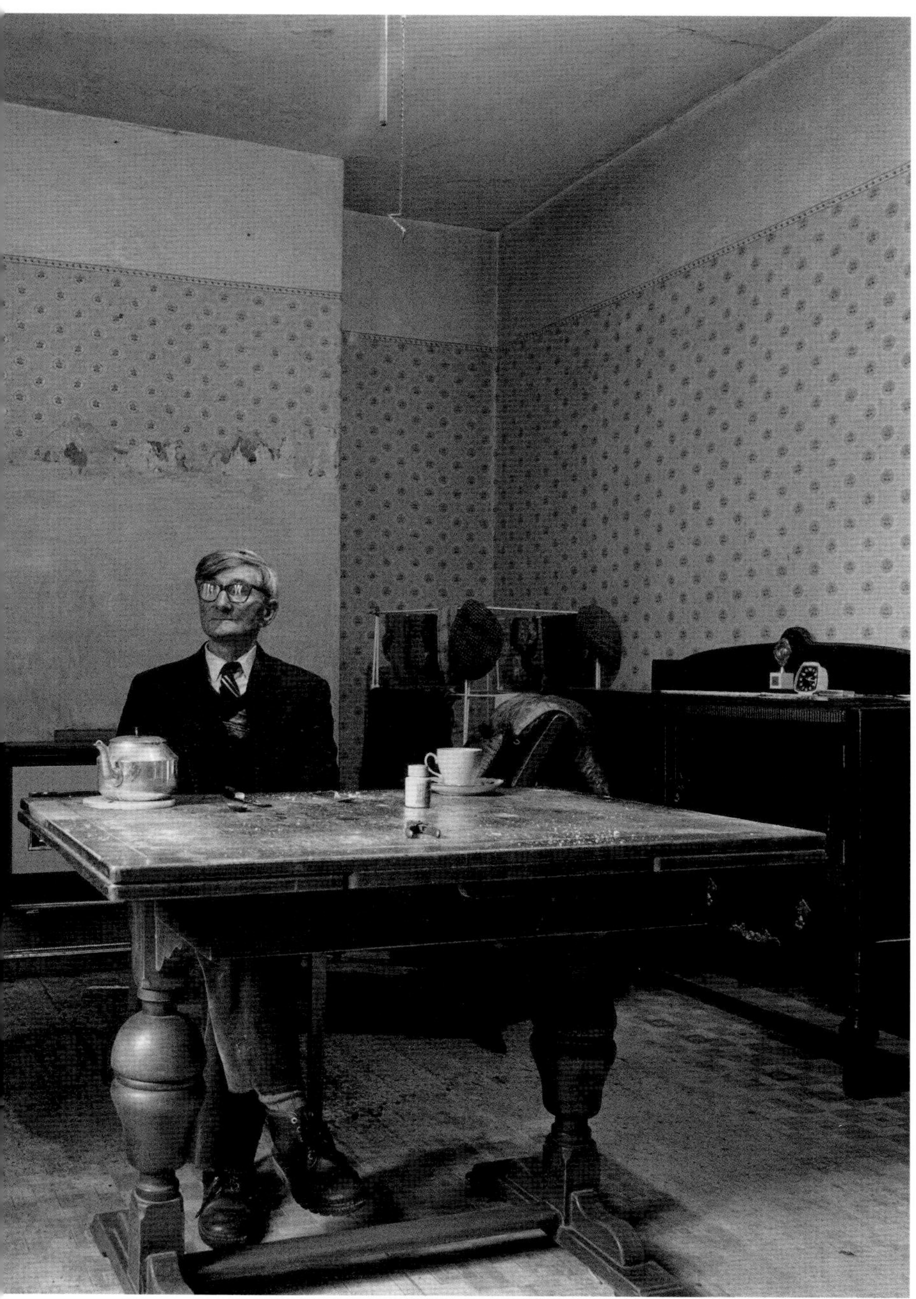

   Jimmy Dodds (Byker) 1980

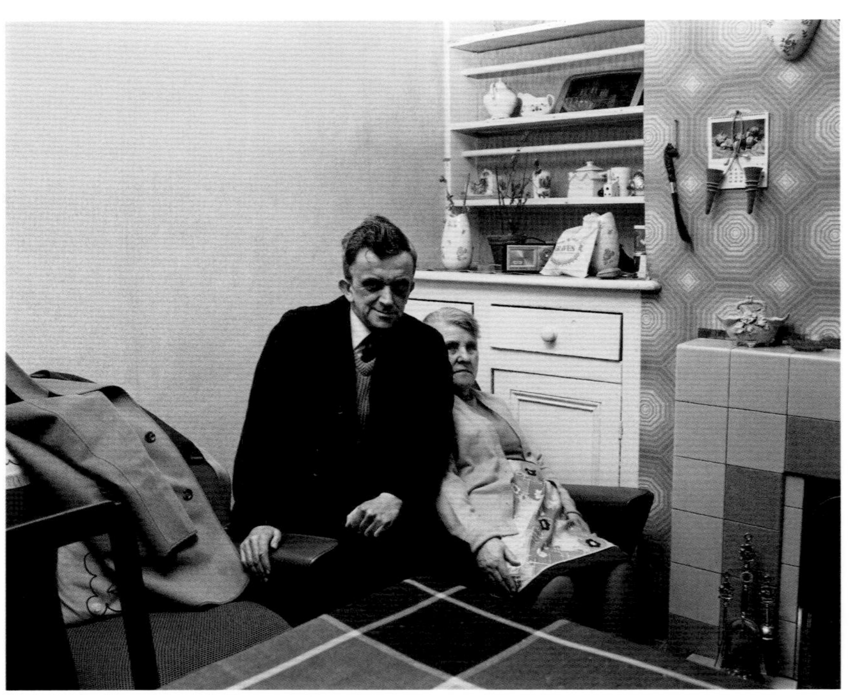

   Richard and Winifred Graham, Byker 1974

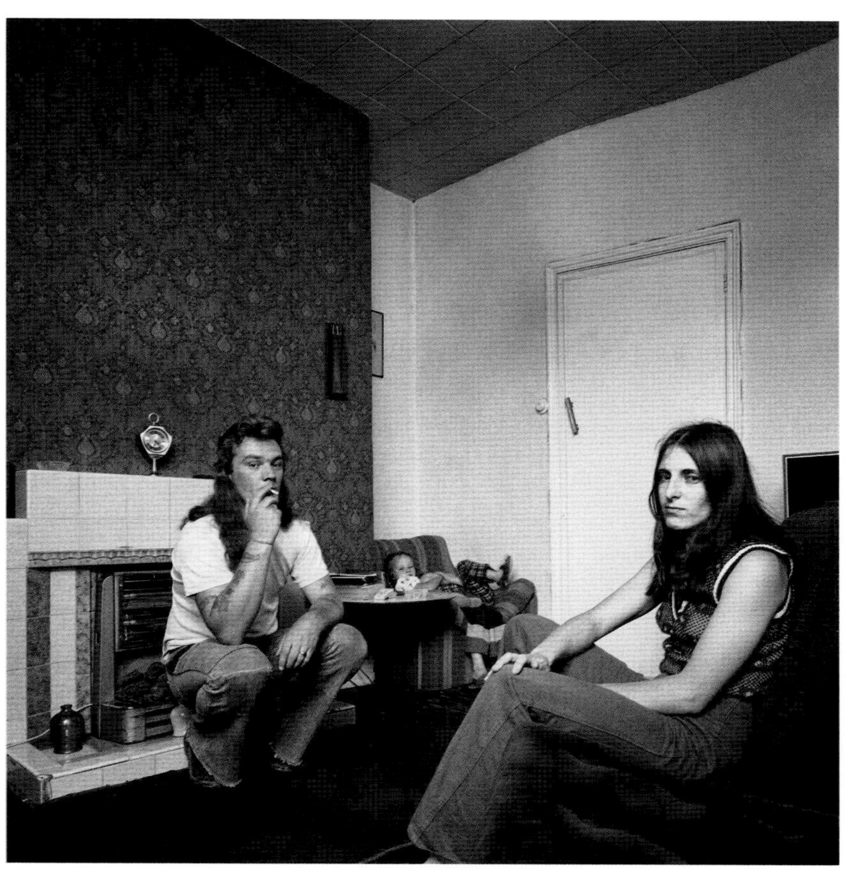

  Gillian and Eddie Robson, Byker 1975

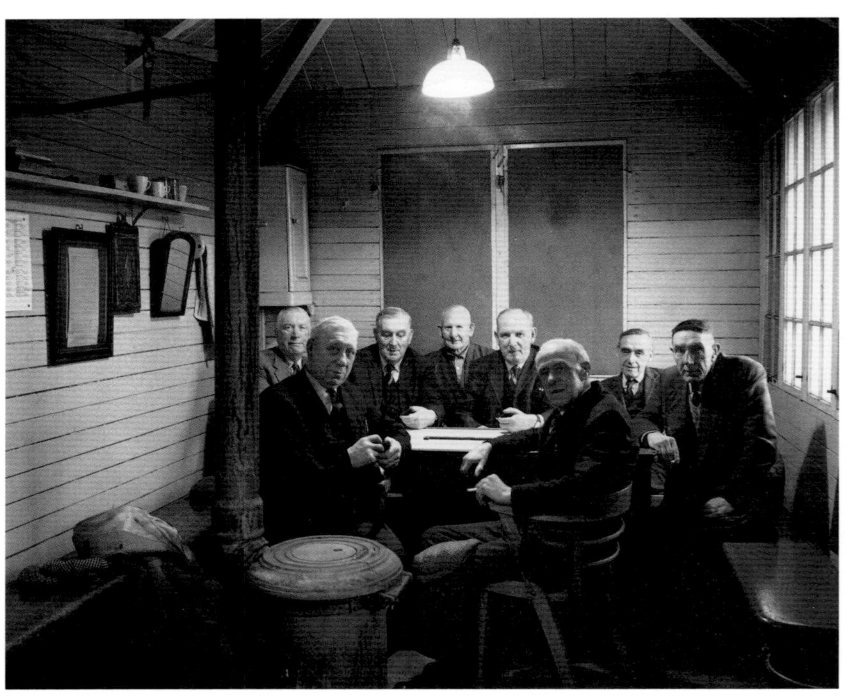

   Byker Park Dominoes Club (Byker) 1974

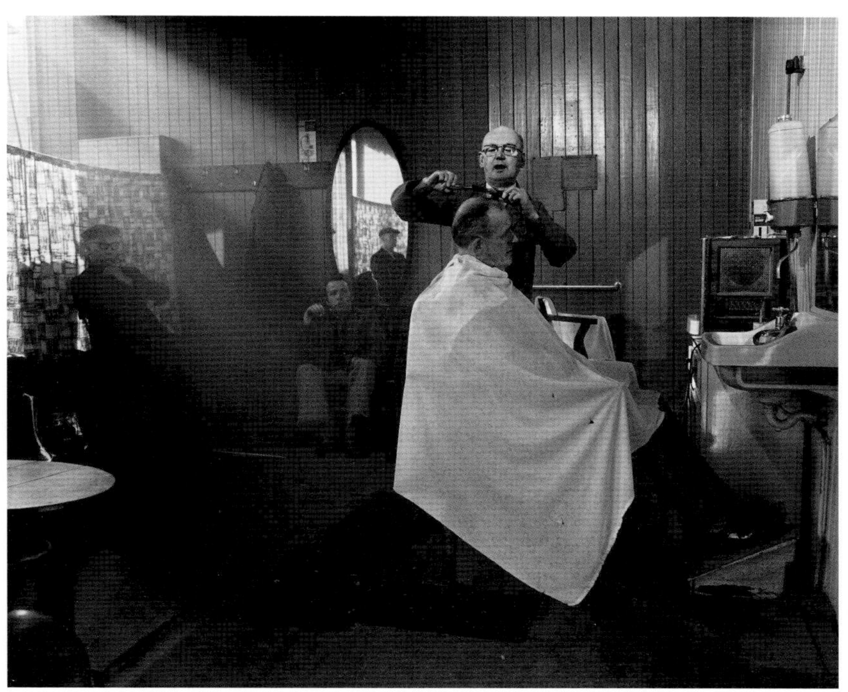

 W.H. Douglas - Gents Hairdresser (Byker) 1974

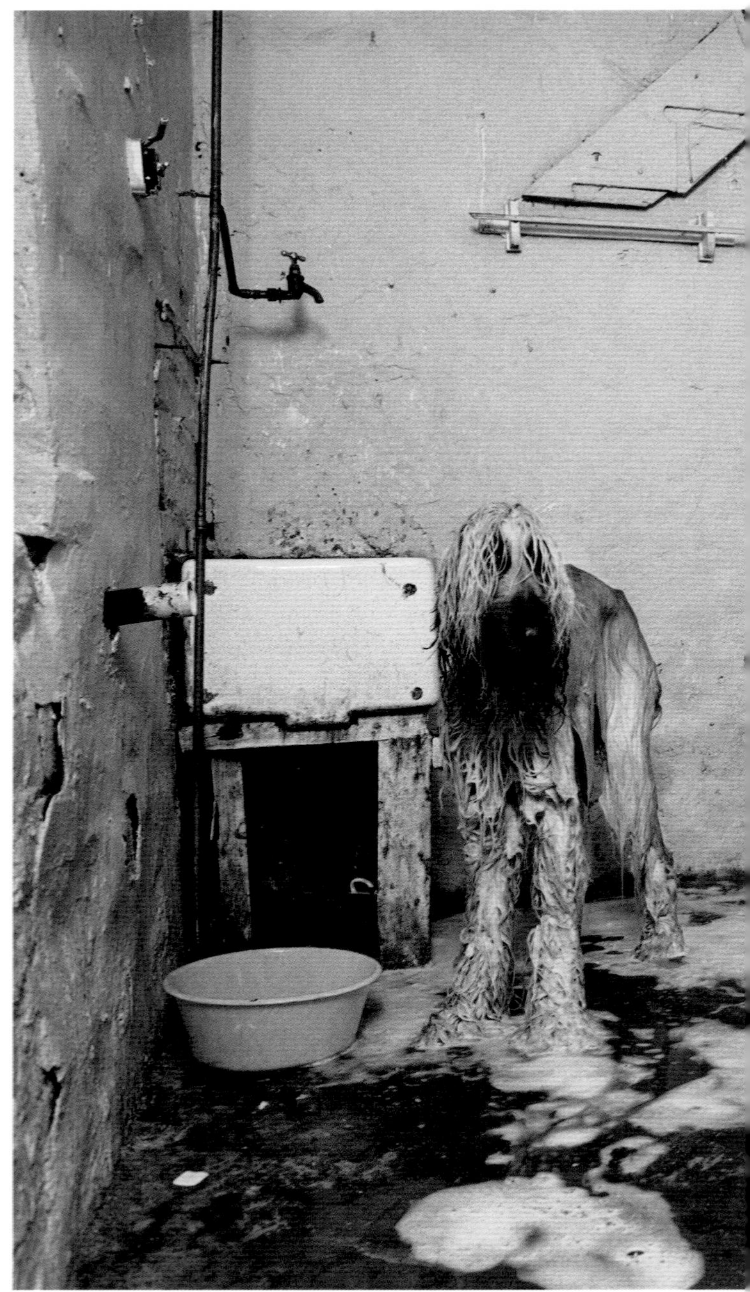

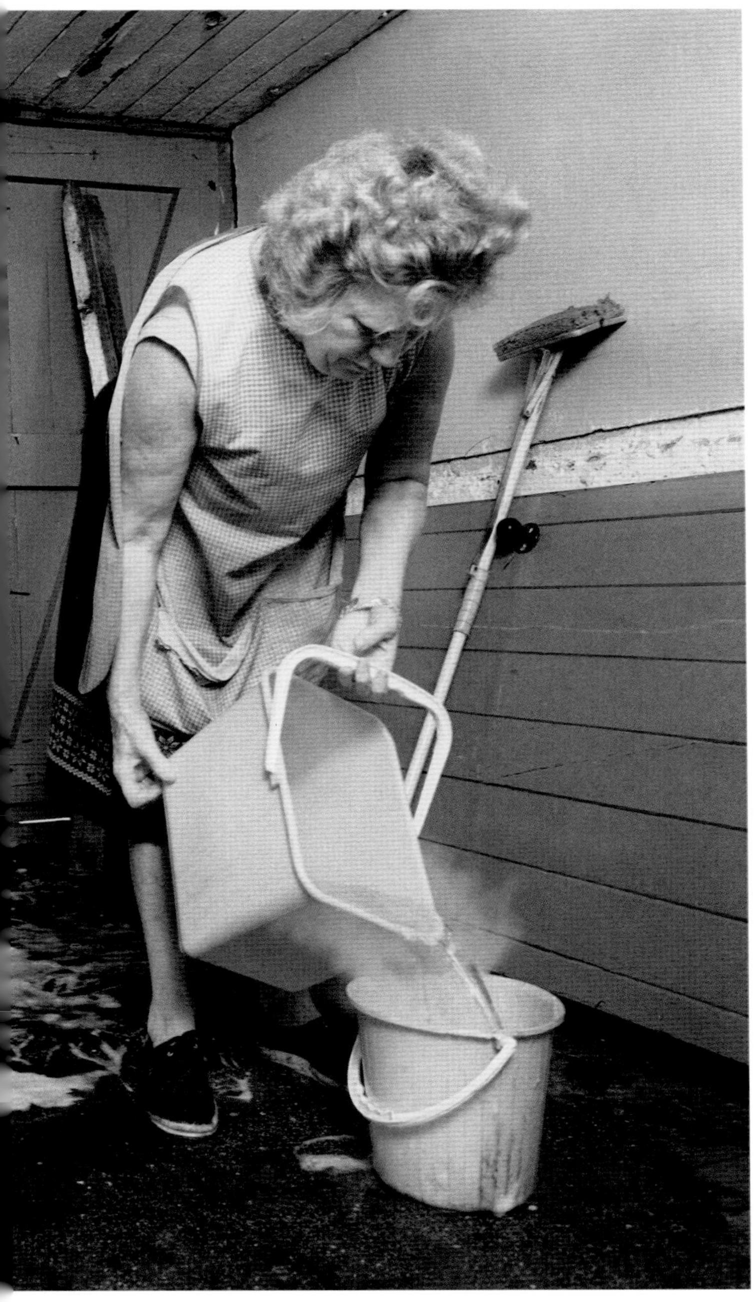

   Dogs Hairdressing, Shields Road (Byker) 1981

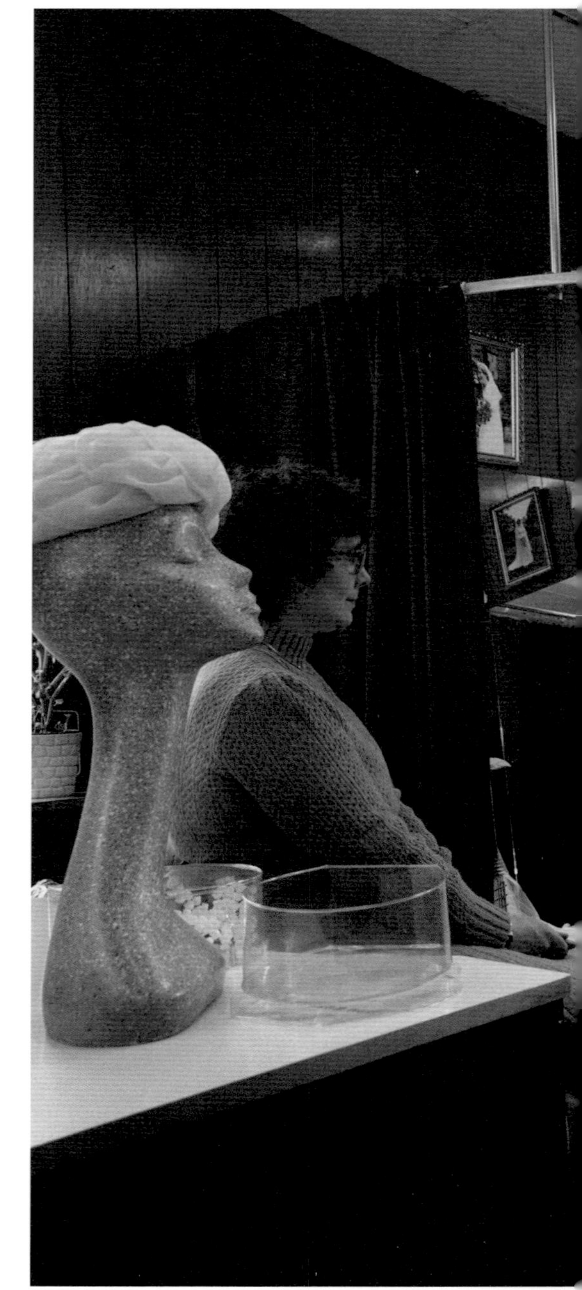

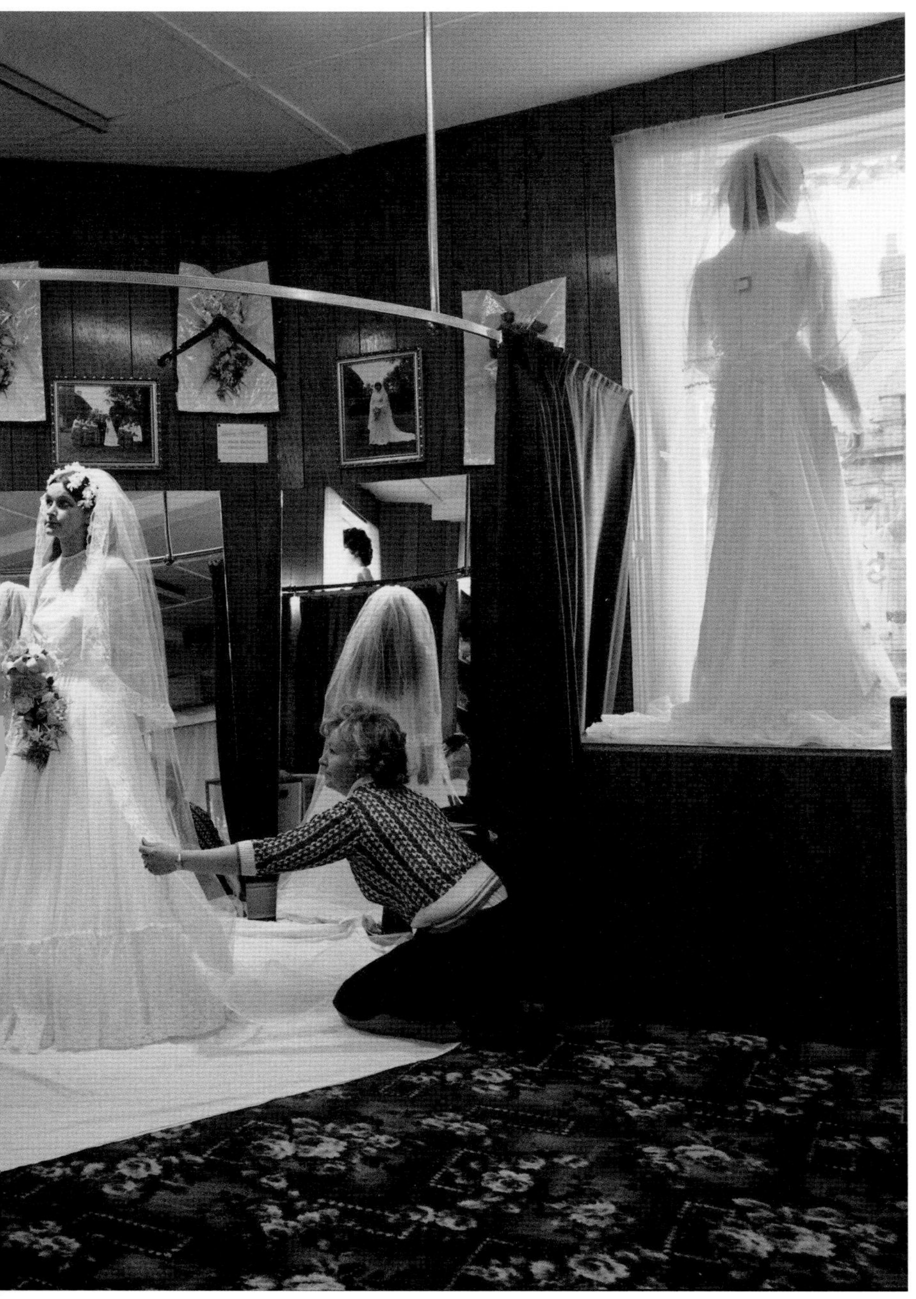

    Bridal Bar, Shields Road, Byker 1981

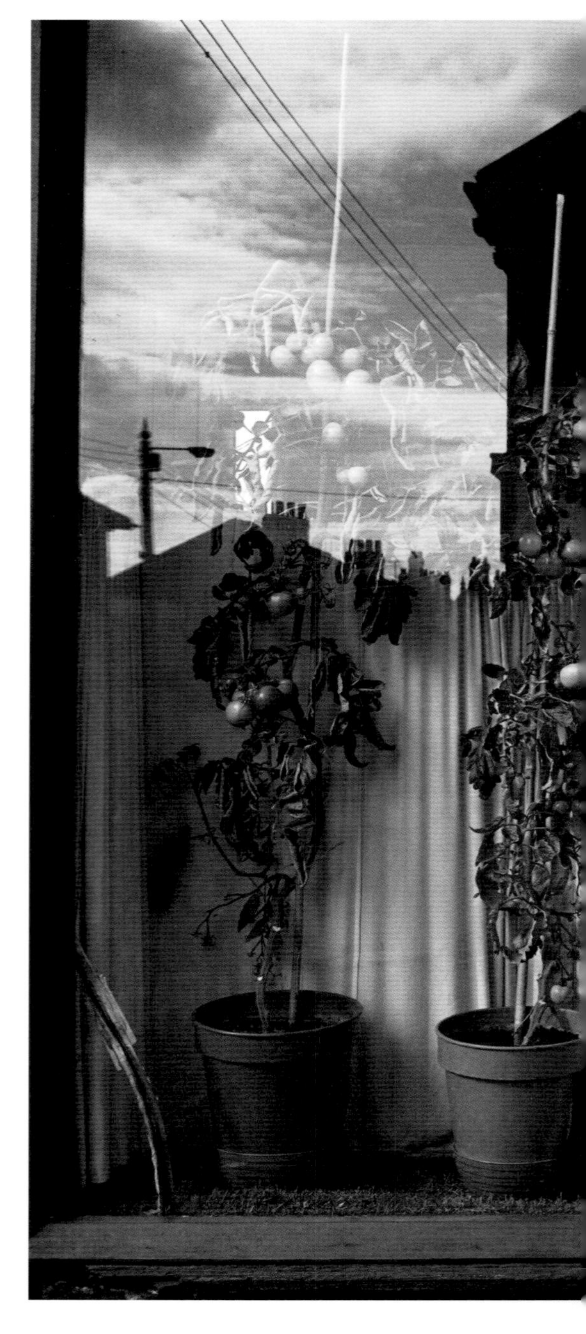

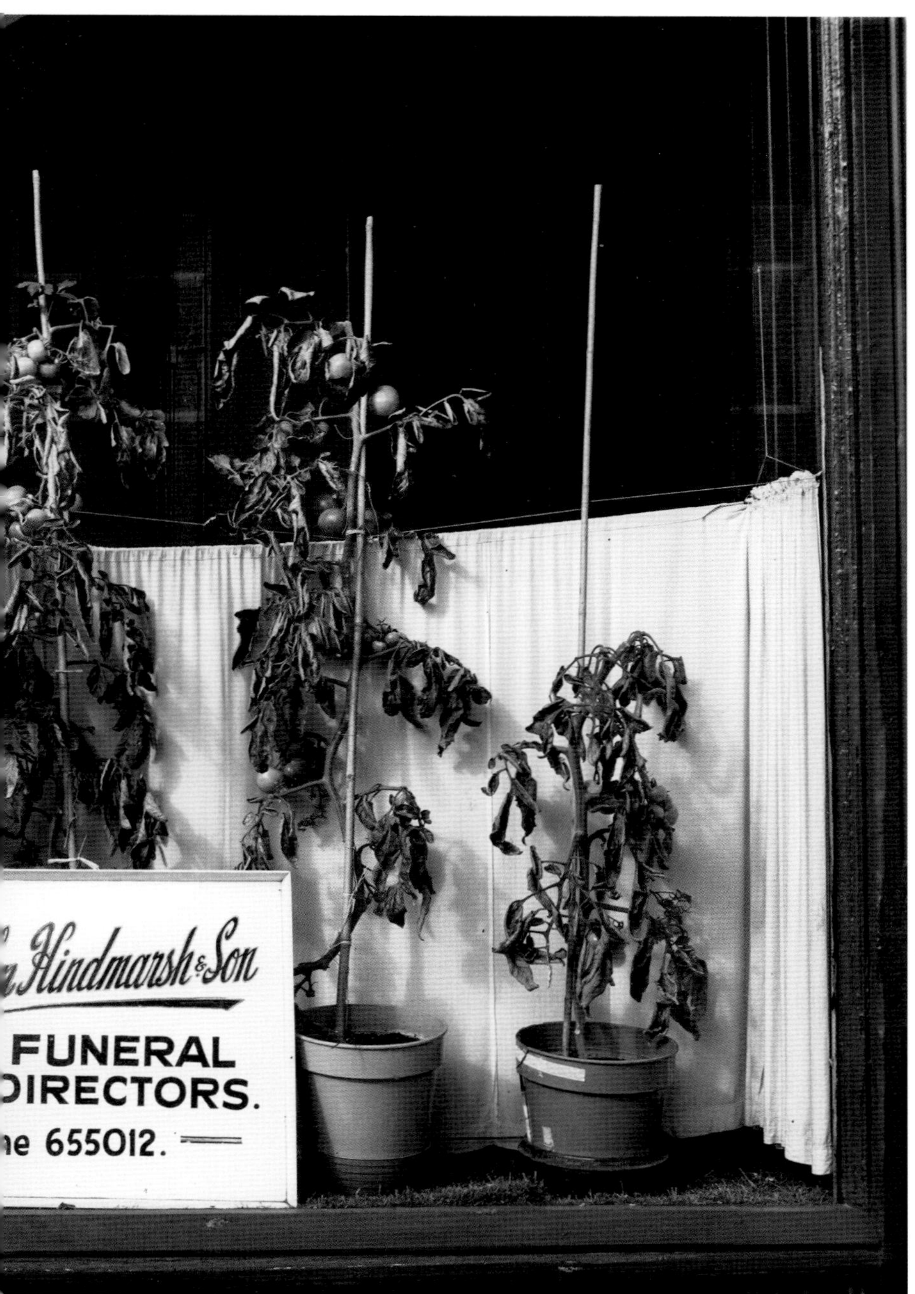

   John Hindmarsh & Son, Funeral Directors', Raby Street (Byker) 1974

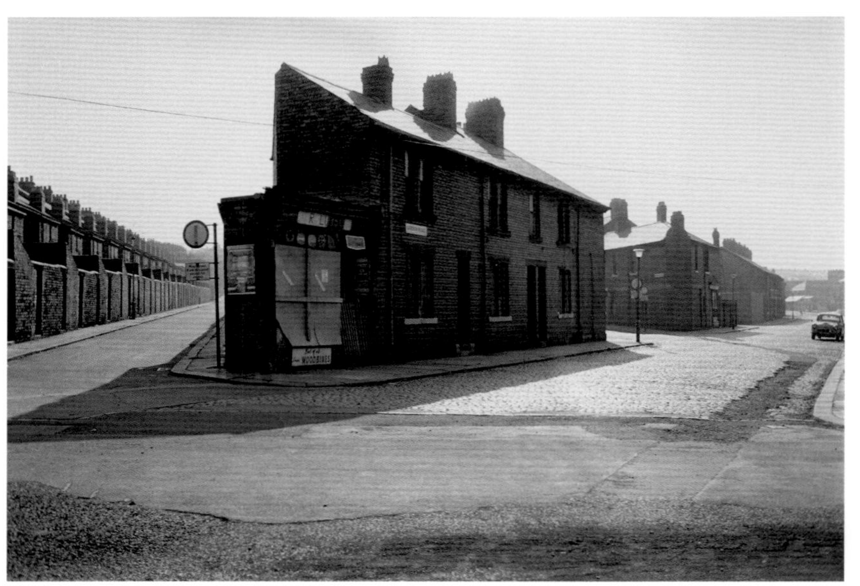

48   *Gordon Road (Byker)* 1971

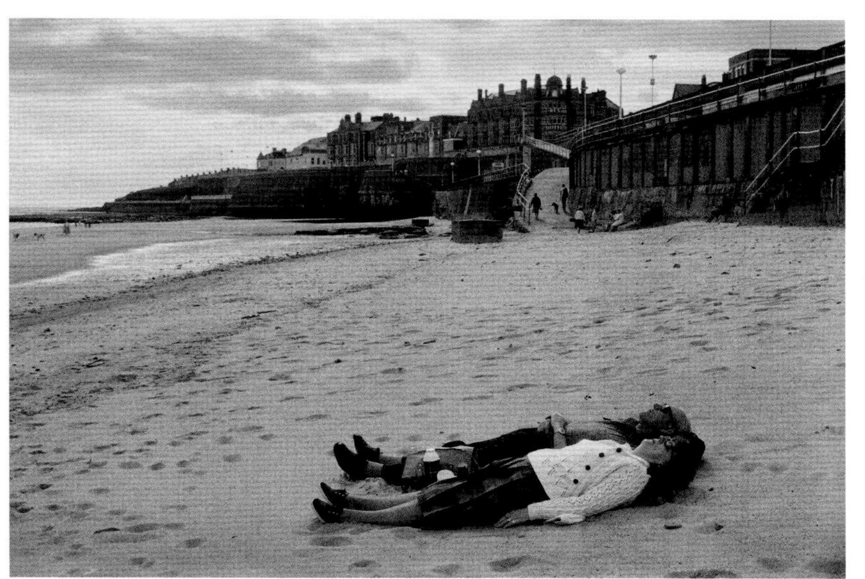

51   *Whitley Bay, August 1985*

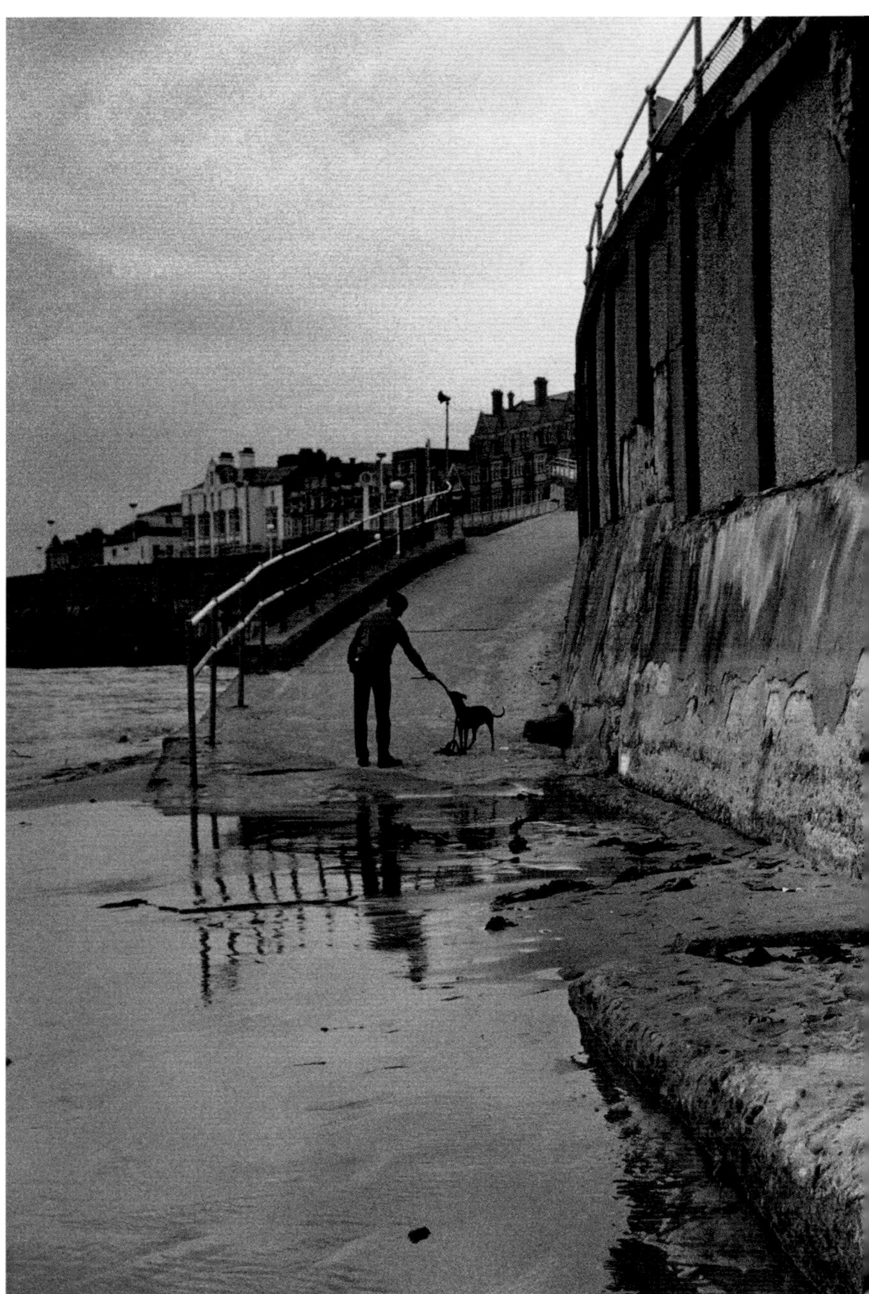

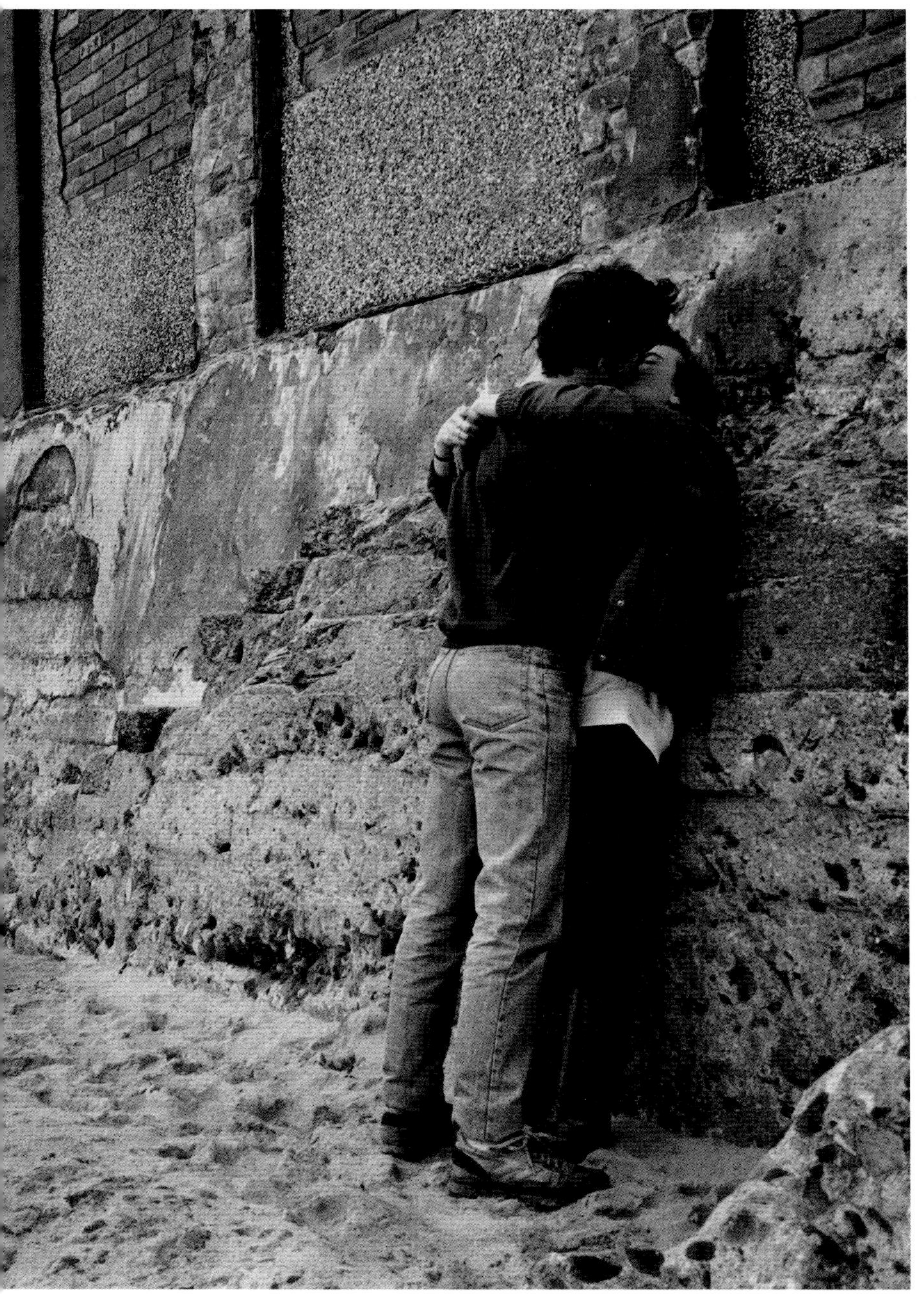

  Whitley Bay, September 1987

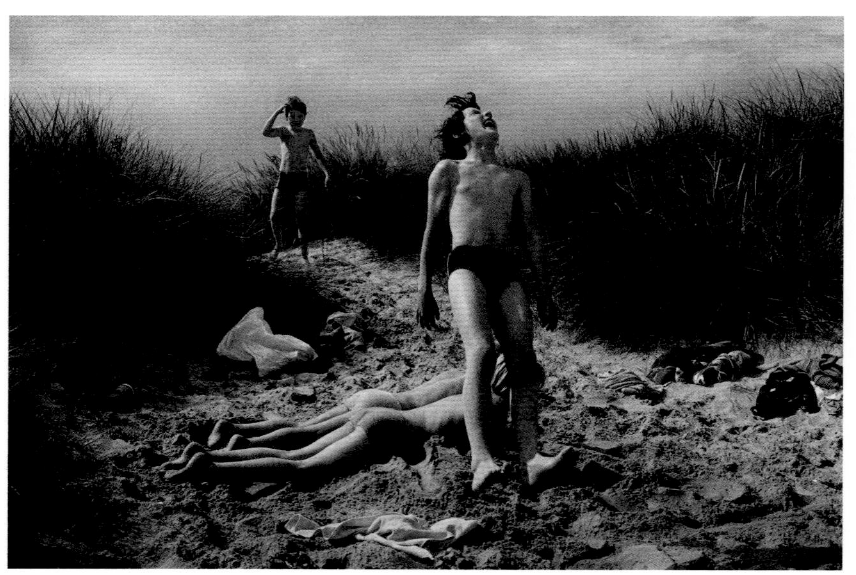

54   *Blyth, August 1978*

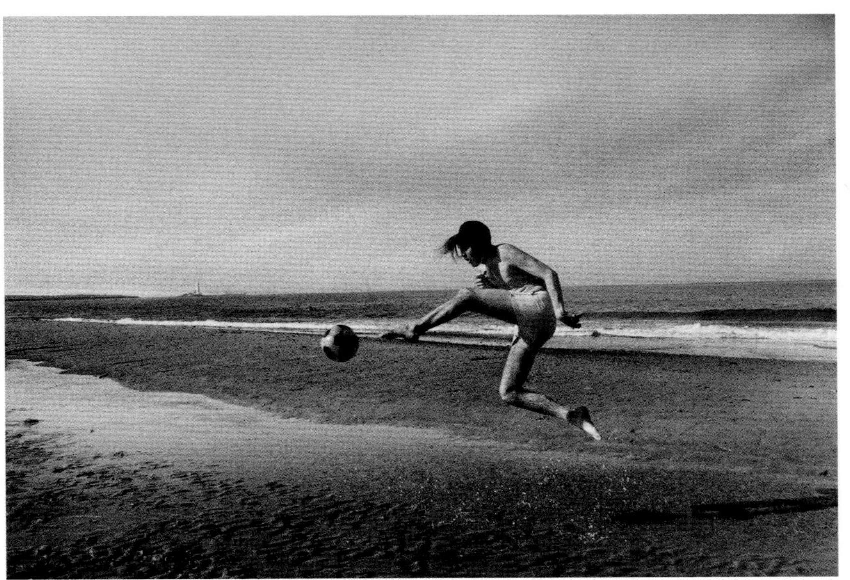

  Whitley Bay, June 1989

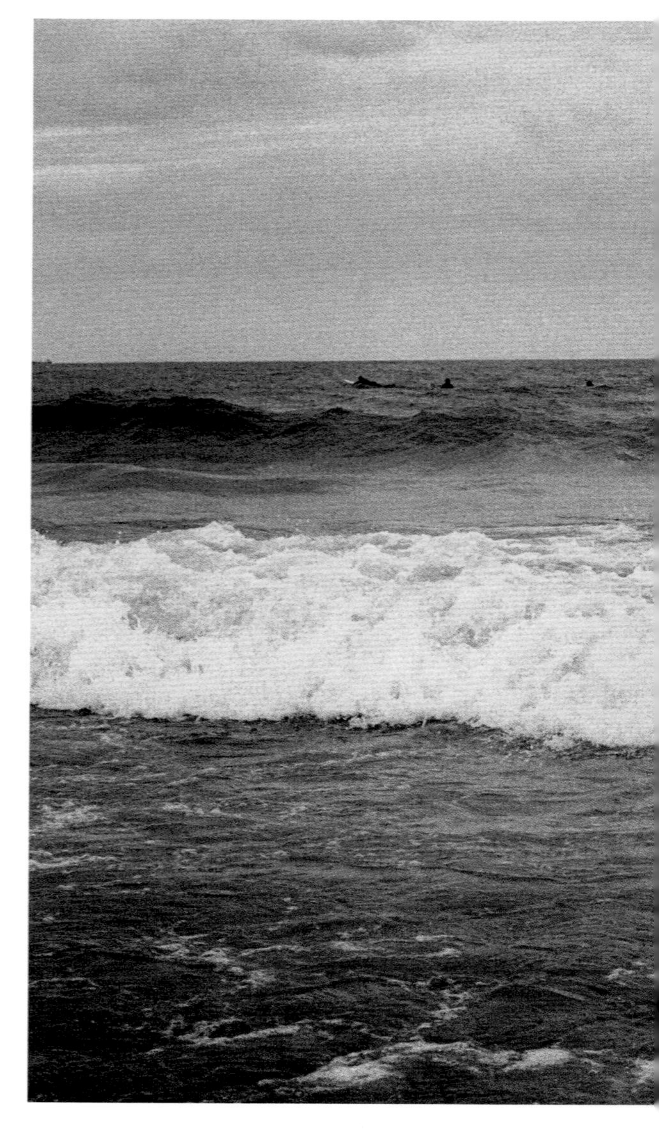

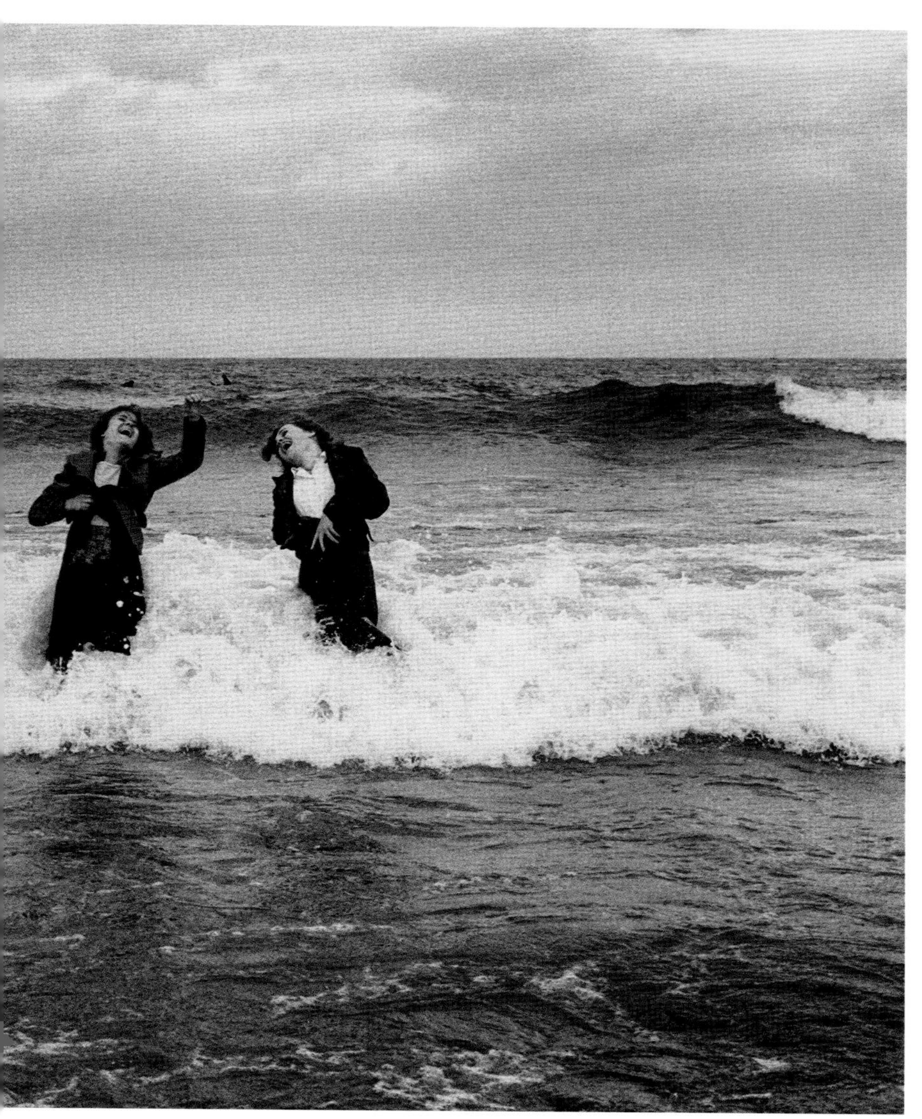

     Whitley Bay, August 1985

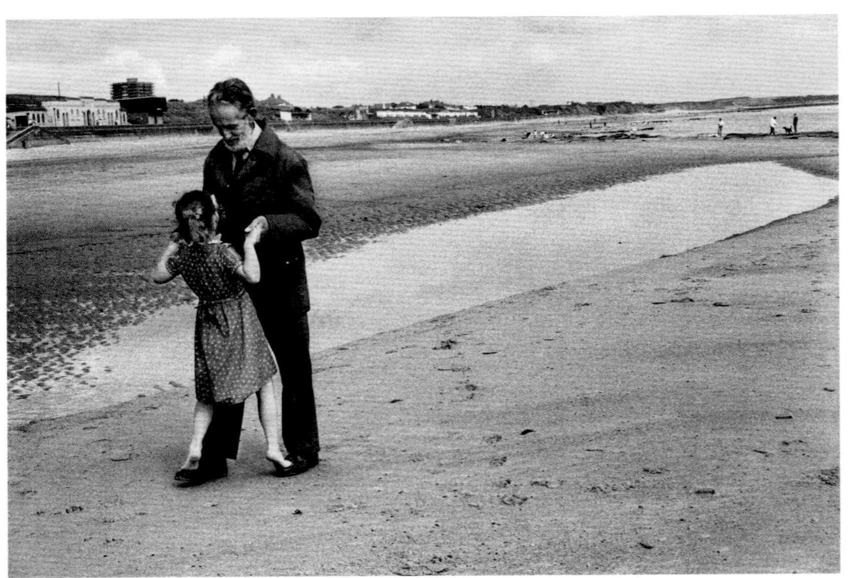

     Whitley Bay, August 1990

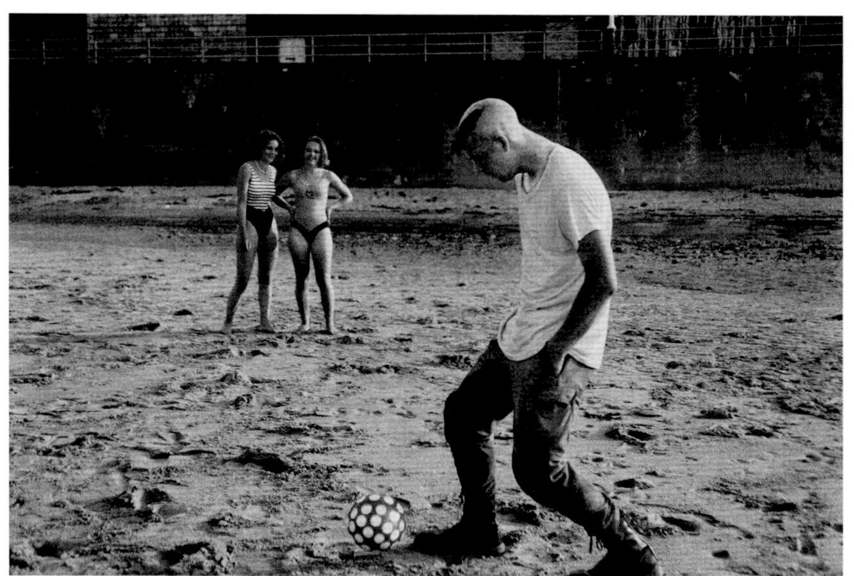

   Whitely Bay, June 1989

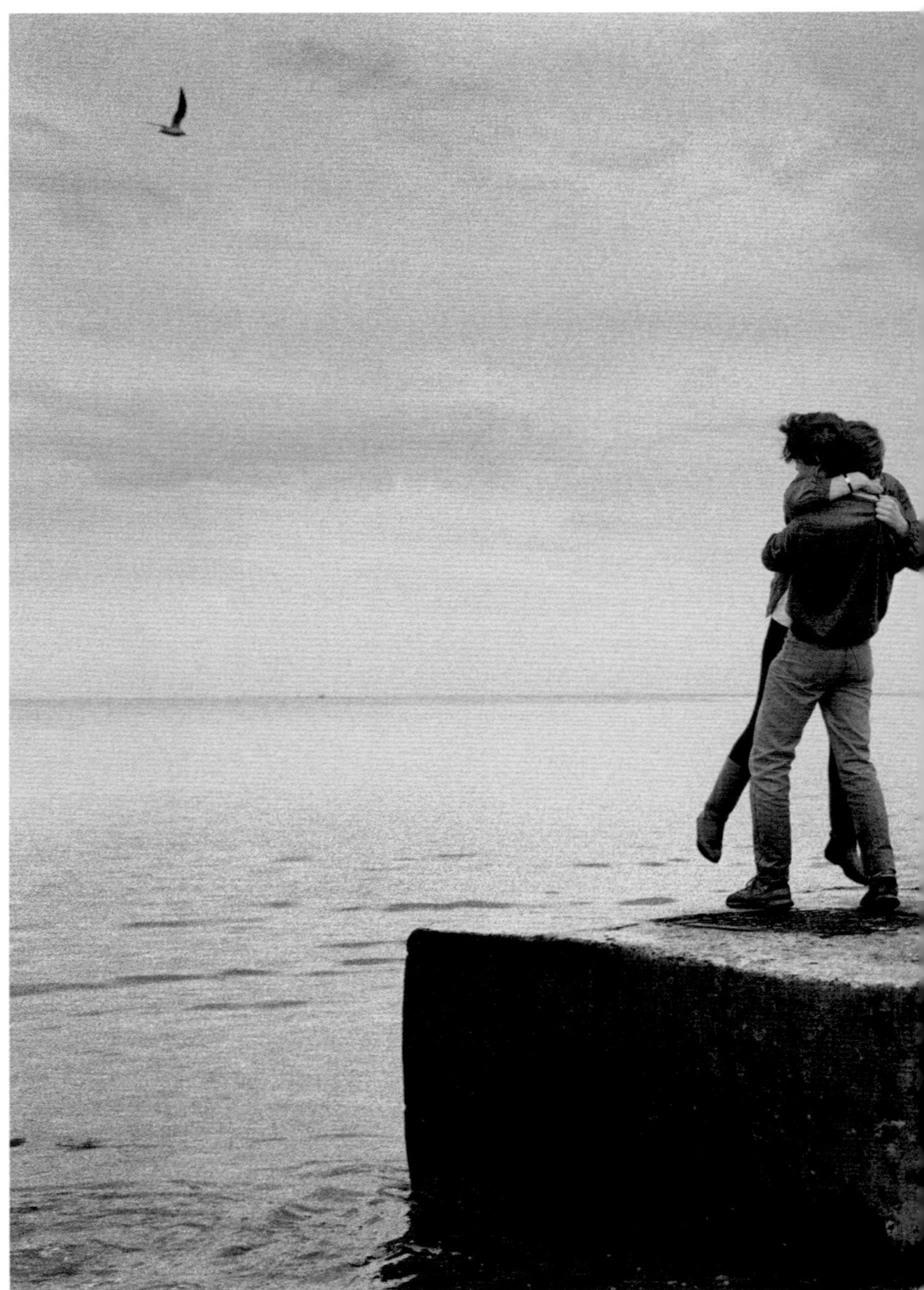

    Whitley Bay, August 1985

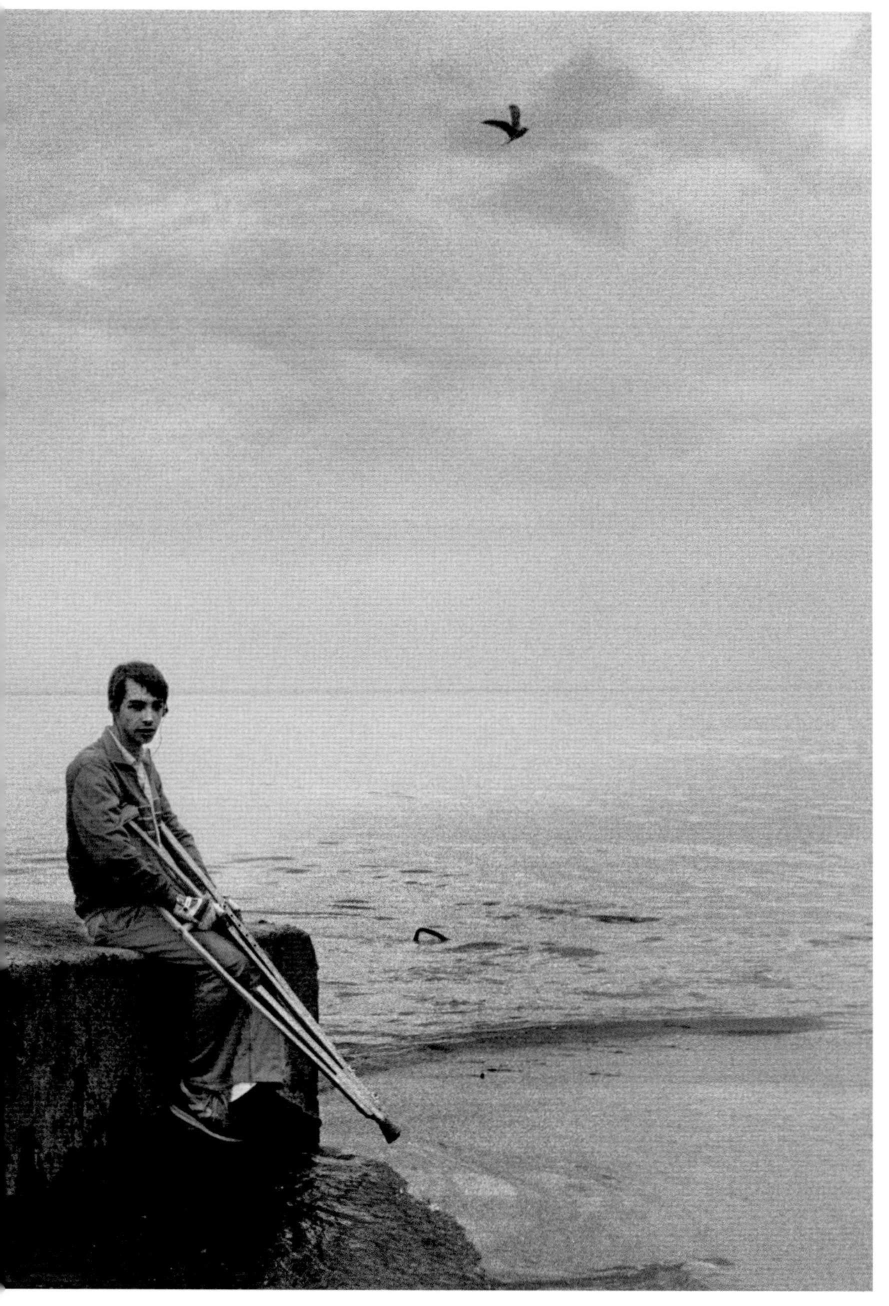

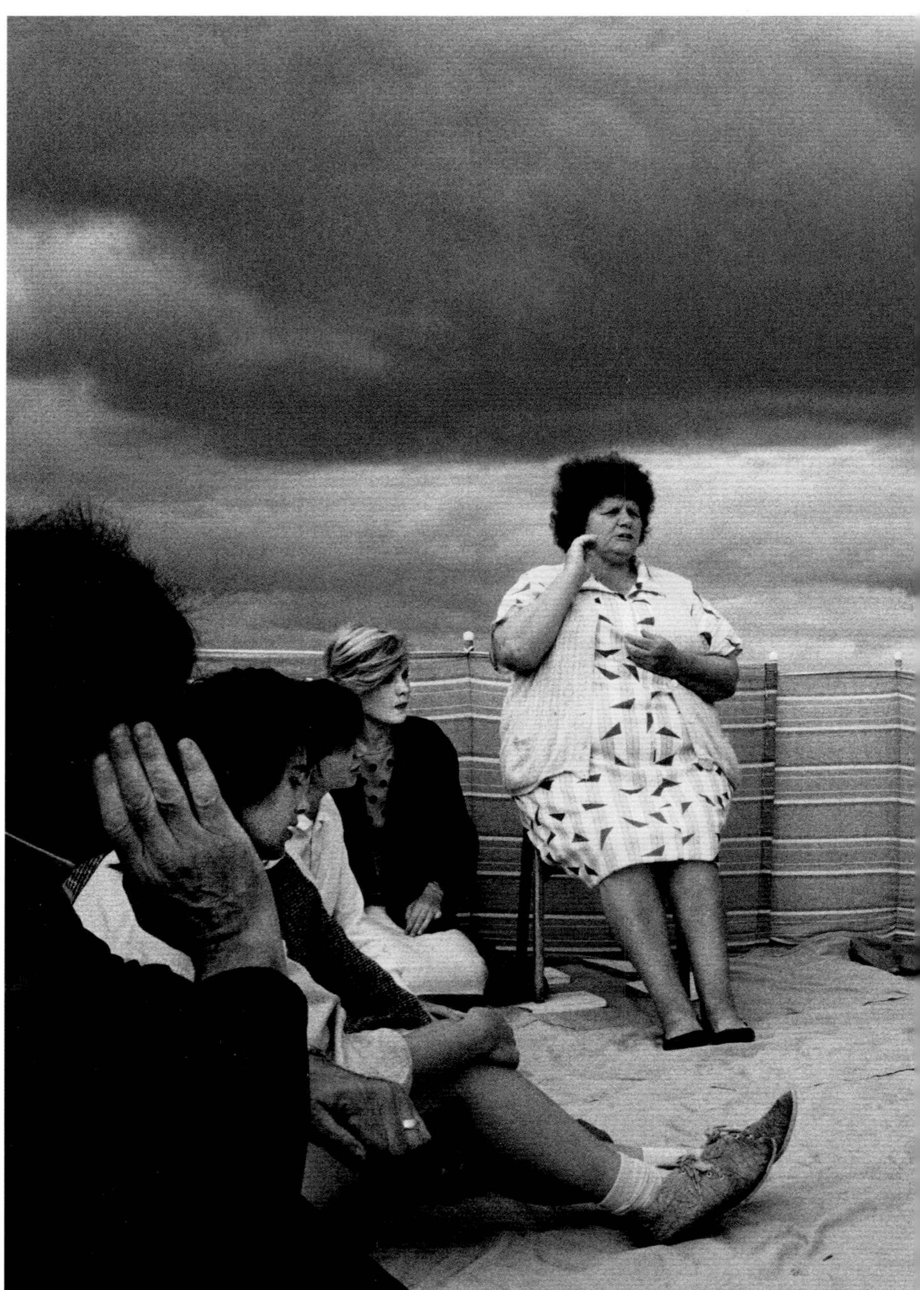

     Whitley Bay, August 1986

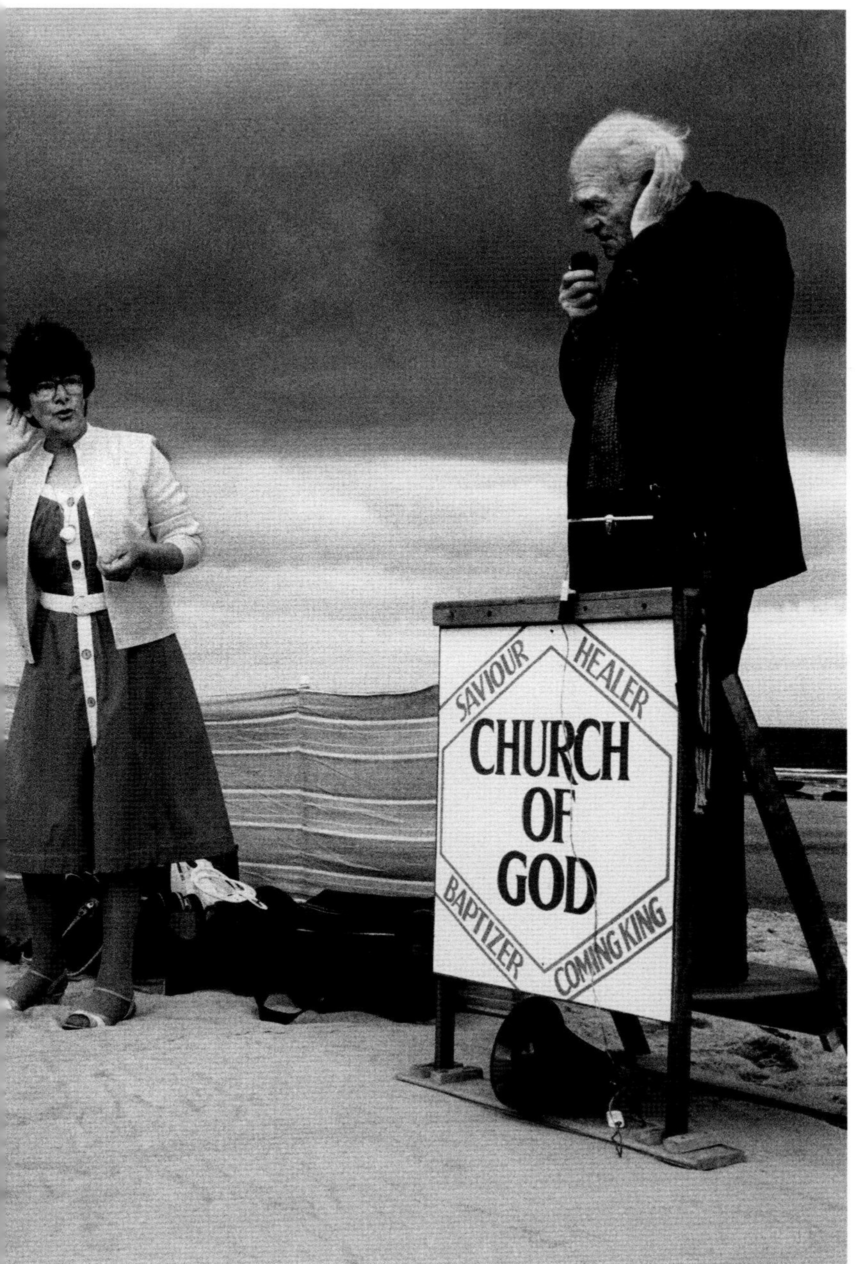

SAVIOUR
HEALER
CHURCH
OF
GOD
BAPTIZER
COMING KING

SIRKKA-LIISA KONTTINEN

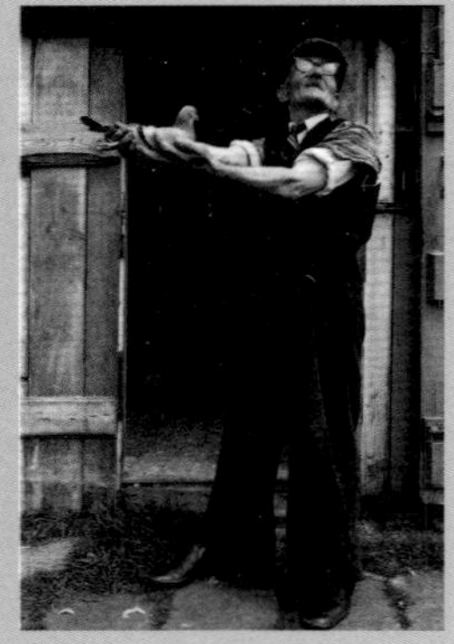

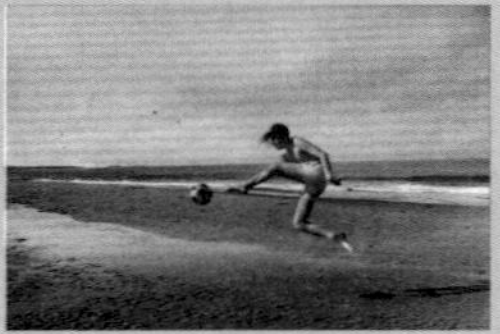

'Before I ever thought of a project, I began photographing whatever struck me as beautiful, amazing, worth telling about … In all of my work, testimonies have been an important element of the projects.'

Born in Finland, Sirkka-Liisa Konttinen studied in London, founding the Amber Film & Photography Collective with her fellow students, before they moved to Newcastle upon Tyne together in the 1960s. She has been based in the North East of England ever since, deeply rooted in the local community.

Focusing on two of her photographic series – *Byker* and *Writing in the Sand* – this book captures the inner city working-class community in Byker and its access to leisure by the sea. It not only reveals the devastating impact that the redevelopment of Newcastle's East End had on its people, but also conversely shows scenes of joy – from children playing in the street to group outings to the beach.

Konttinen's love for this part of the world is at the heart of these moving but never sentimental pictures. Her photographs and Amber's films were inscribed in the British section of the UNESCO Memory of the World Register in 2011.

1:       Community and Solidarity

1:1   **LIZ JOHNSON ARTUR**
1:2   **SIRKKA-LIISA KONTTINEN**
1:3   **SABELO MLANGENI**
1:4   **SHEBA CHHACHHI**

UK £12.00 US $17.99 CAN $22.99

ISBN 978-1-84976-800-9

9 781849 768009

Tate Photography Series

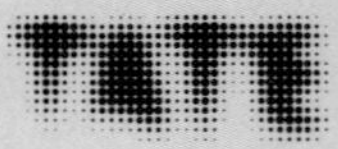

CLAUDIA ANDUJAR

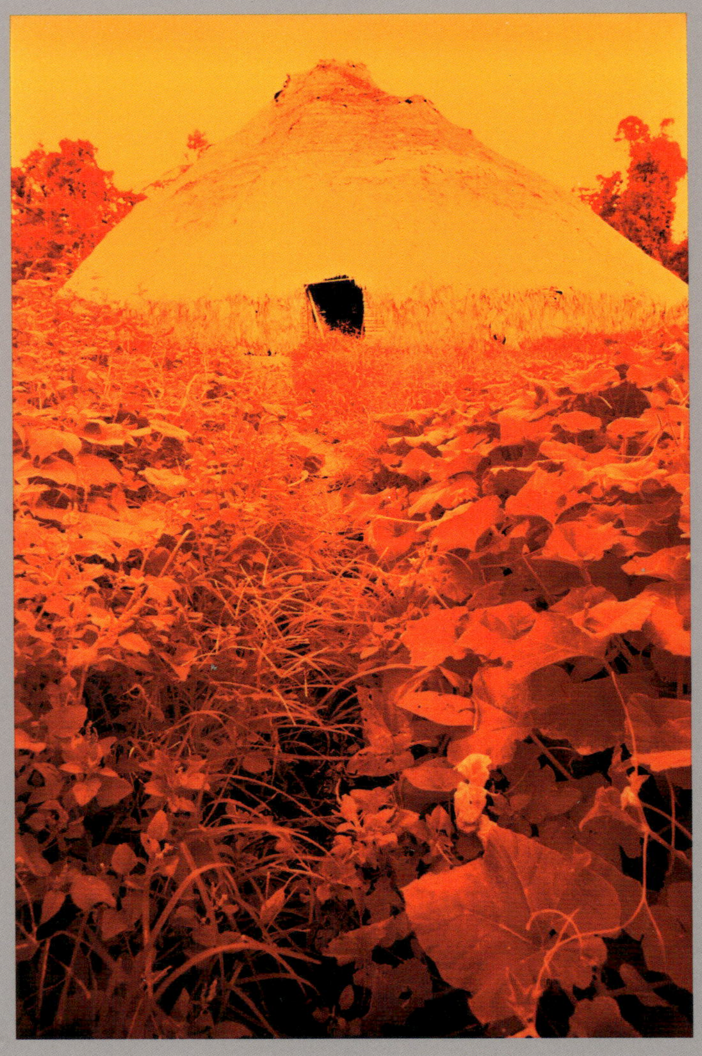